Celia Cruz: The Defiant Voice of Afro-Cuban Music

ROBERTO MIGUEL RODRIGUEZ

2023

1

Copyright Page

TITLE: Celia Cruz: The Defiant Voice of Afro-Cuban Music

1ST Edition

Copyright @ 2023

Roberto M. Rodriguez. All rights reserved.

ISBN: 9798223337553

Table of Contents

Title Page 1

Celia Cruz: The Defiant Voice of Afro-Cuban Music............................7

Chapter 1: Celia Cruz: Biography of the Afro-Cuban Singer Who Refused to Sing for Dictator Fidel Castro 8

Chapter 2: Afro-Cuban Music: Exploring the Impact of Afro-Cuban Music on Celia Cruz's Career and her Contributions to the Genre..... 19

Chapter 3: Political Activism: Analyzing Celia Cruz's Refusal to Sing for Fidel Castro and Exploring her Role as a Political Activist....................27

Chapter 4: Latin American Divas: Examining Celia Cruz's Influence on the Rise of Latin American Female Singers and her Impact on the Diva Culture 36

Chapter 5: Cuban Exile Experience: Investigating the Experiences of Cuban Exiles, including Celia Cruz, and their Impact on their Artistic Expressions 44

Chapter 6: Afro-Latina Identity: Discussing Celia Cruz's Afro-Latina Identity and its Significance in her Music and Activism 52

Chapter 7: Women in Music: Exploring the Challenges Faced by Women in the Music Industry through the Lens of Celia Cruz's Career 58

Chapter 8: Cultural Resistance: Analyzing how Celia Cruz's Refusal to Perform for Fidel Castro was an Act of Cultural Resistance against the Cuban Regime... 66

Chapter 9: Music and Migration: Examining the Influence of Migration on Celia Cruz's Music and her Experiences as a Migrant Artist............ 72

Chapter 10: Afro-Caribbean Influences: Investigating the Afro-Caribbean Musical Influences in Celia Cruz's Work and their Impact on her Style... 78

Chapter 11: Legacy and Impact: Discussing the Lasting Legacy of Celia Cruz and her Impact on the Afro-Cuban Music Scene and Beyond.... 85

Celia Cruz: The Defiant Voice of Afro-Cuban Music

By Roberto Miguel Rodriguez

Chapter 1: Celia Cruz: Biography of the Afro-Cuban Singer Who Refused to Sing for Dictator Fidel Castro

Early Life and Musical Beginnings

Celia Cruz, the legendary Afro-Cuban singer, was born on October 21, 1925, in Havana, Cuba. From an early age, she showed a natural talent for singing and a deep connection to Afro-Cuban music. Growing up in a vibrant neighborhood, she was immersed in the rich musical traditions of her Afro-Caribbean heritage.

Cruz's musical journey began in her childhood, singing at local gatherings and family events. Despite her parents' initial disapproval of her pursuit of a career in music, she persevered, fueled by her relentless passion for singing. Her determination and talent caught the attention of local musicians, and at the age of just sixteen, she joined the popular Cuban music group, La Sonora Matancera.

Joining La Sonora Matancera marked a turning point in Cruz's life. The group exposed her to a wider audience and allowed her to explore different musical styles. With her powerful voice and dynamic stage presence, she quickly became a beloved figure in the Afro-Cuban music scene. Her distinct vocal style, filled with emotion and energy, captivated audiences and earned her the title of the "Queen of Salsa."

As her career blossomed, Cruz faced numerous obstacles and challenges. Her refusal to sing for dictator Fidel Castro, a bold act of political activism, made her a symbol of resistance against the Cuban regime. Despite facing backlash and threats, she remained steadfast in her beliefs and used her platform to advocate for freedom and democracy.

Cruz's influence extended beyond the realm of politics. She paved the way for Latin American female singers, breaking down barriers and challenging societal norms. Her vibrant personality and extravagant stage costumes also contributed to the rise of the diva culture, inspiring countless artists to embrace their own uniqueness and celebrate their identities.

Throughout her life, Cruz never forgot her roots. As a Cuban exile, she understood the pain and struggle of her fellow countrymen, and her music became a powerful expression of the Cuban exile experience. She used her platform to shed light on the injustices faced by Cuban exiles and to preserve the rich cultural heritage of her homeland.

Cruz's Afro-Latina identity was central to her music and activism. She embraced her African heritage and celebrated the diversity of Latin American culture. Through her songs, she empowered Afro-Caribbean communities and challenged societal prejudices, leaving a lasting impact on the Afro-Cuban music scene and beyond.

Celia Cruz's legacy is undeniable. Her music continues to inspire and captivate audiences worldwide. Her refusal to perform for Fidel Castro was not just an act of defiance, but a powerful statement of cultural resistance. She used her voice to fight for justice, equality, and freedom, leaving behind a lasting legacy as one of the greatest Afro-Cuban singers of all time.

Rise to Fame in Cuba

In the subchapter titled "Rise to Fame in Cuba," we delve into the early years of Celia Cruz's career and her ascent to stardom in her home country. Born in Havana, Cuba, Celia Cruz was a force to be reckoned with, defying societal norms and breaking barriers that hindered her dreams.

Cruz's journey began in the vibrant streets of Havana, where she discovered her passion for singing at a young age. With her powerful voice and undeniable talent, she quickly became a local sensation, captivating audiences with her electrifying performances. Her Afro-Cuban roots heavily influenced her music, incorporating elements of Afro-Caribbean rhythms and traditional Cuban melodies.

As her popularity grew, Cruz became a symbol of strength and resilience for the Afro-Cuban community. Her refusal to sing for the dictator Fidel Castro showcased her unwavering commitment to her principles and her dedication to fighting for the rights of her people. This act of defiance solidified her role as a political activist, using her platform to advocate for change and shed light on the struggles faced by the Cuban people.

Cruz's rise to fame in Cuba was not without its challenges. As a woman in the music industry, she faced numerous obstacles and prejudices. However, her unwavering determination and unmatched talent allowed her to break through these barriers and pave the way for future generations of female artists.

Her influence extended far beyond the borders of Cuba, reshaping the Latin American music industry and inspiring a new generation of divas. Through her dynamic performances, Cruz became an icon of empowerment, proving that women could dominate the stage and command the respect they deserved.

Her experiences as a Cuban exile also played a significant role in shaping her artistic expressions. The hardships faced by Cruz and other exiles fueled her passion for creating music that captured the essence of their shared experiences, giving a voice to those who had been silenced.

Cruz's Afro-Latina identity was a central theme in her music and activism, celebrating her African heritage and embracing her roots. Her songs became anthems of pride, empowering Afro-Latinos around the world and challenging societal norms of beauty and identity.

Today, Celia Cruz's legacy lives on, her impact on the Afro-Cuban music scene and beyond remaining unparalleled. Her defiance against the Cuban regime and her unwavering commitment to her art continue to inspire artists and activists alike. Through her music, she created a bridge between cultures, uniting people through the universal language of music.

In the next chapter, we will explore the challenges faced by women in the music industry, as seen through the lens of Celia Cruz's remarkable career. Stay tuned as we delve deeper into the struggles and triumphs of this extraordinary woman.

Cuban Revolution and Celia's Decision to Leave

In this subchapter, we delve into the turbulent times of the Cuban Revolution and explore Celia Cruz's decision to leave her home country. The chapter highlights the impact of the revolution on the Afro-Cuban music scene and Celia's role as a defiant voice against the dictatorship of Fidel Castro.

The Cuban Revolution, led by Fidel Castro, brought about significant changes to the socio-political landscape of Cuba. As the country transitioned into a communist regime, censorship and control over artistic expression became the norm. Artists were expected to align themselves with the revolution and its ideals, which posed a dilemma for Celia Cruz.

Celia, known as the Queen of Salsa, was a proud Afro-Cuban singer whose music celebrated her African roots. However, she refused to compromise her artistic integrity and refused to sing for Fidel Castro. This decision was a bold act of political activism, and it solidified Celia's position as a symbol of resistance against the regime.

Leaving her beloved homeland was not an easy decision for Celia. She had to leave behind her family, friends, and the vibrant Afro-Cuban music scene that had shaped her career. Yet, her departure marked a turning point in her life, as she embarked on a journey that would ultimately lead her to international fame and recognition.

Celia's decision to leave Cuba was not only a personal one but also a reflection of the experiences of many Cuban exiles. Through her music and performances, Celia became the voice of the Cuban diaspora, expressing the pain, longing, and resilience of those who had been uprooted from their homeland.

Furthermore, Celia's Afro-Latina identity played a significant role in her music and activism. As an Afro-Cuban woman, she faced discrimination and prejudice throughout her career. However, she embraced her heritage and used her platform to celebrate Afro-Caribbean culture, challenging societal norms and stereotypes.

Celia's refusal to perform for Fidel Castro was more than just a personal decision; it was an act of cultural resistance. By standing up against the oppressive regime, she demonstrated the power of music as a tool for political change and the importance of artistic freedom.

In conclusion, the Cuban Revolution and Celia's decision to leave her homeland shaped her career and activism in profound ways. By exploring this chapter, readers will gain a deeper understanding of the impact of political turmoil on artists, the challenges faced by women in the music industry, and the role of music as a form of resistance. Celia Cruz's story serves as an inspiration, reminding us of the enduring legacy of a woman who refused to be silenced and whose music continues to resonate with audiences around the world.

Exile in the United States

Celia Cruz: The Defiant Voice of Afro-Cuban Music

Exile in the United States is a pivotal chapter in the life of Celia Cruz, the Afro-Cuban singer who refused to sing for dictator Fidel Castro. This chapter explores the challenges faced by Cruz as she navigated her new life in the United States and the profound impact it had on her music and activism.

After Castro's rise to power in Cuba, many artists and intellectuals faced persecution and censorship, forcing them into exile. Cruz, known for her powerful voice and rebellious spirit, chose to leave her beloved homeland rather than compromise her principles. Settling in the United States, she faced the daunting task of rebuilding her career in a foreign land.

The chapter delves into the struggles and triumphs of Cruz during her exile. It examines the experiences of Cuban exiles, including Cruz, and their impact on their artistic expressions. Through interviews with Cruz's friends, collaborators, and fellow exiles, readers gain insight into the challenges faced by those who were forced to leave their homes and start anew.

Moreover, the chapter delves into Cruz's Afro-Latina identity and its significance in her music and activism. As an Afro-Cuban woman in a predominantly white and male-dominated industry, Cruz's journey was fraught with obstacles. She defied societal expectations and embraced her Afro-Cuban roots, becoming a powerful symbol of pride for Afro-Latinas worldwide.

Cruz's refusal to perform for Fidel Castro is analyzed as an act of cultural resistance against the Cuban regime. Her bold stance not only solidified her place as a political activist but also served as an inspiration for others to stand up against oppression. The chapter explores the lasting impact of Cruz's decision on the Afro-Cuban music scene and beyond.

Furthermore, the chapter examines the influence of migration on Cruz's music and her experiences as a migrant artist. It delves into the

Afro-Caribbean musical influences in Cruz's work and their impact on her unique style. Readers gain a deeper understanding of the fusion of African and Latin rhythms that defined Cruz's music and made her a trailblazer in the genre.

Ultimately, this chapter showcases Celia Cruz's defiance, resilience, and unwavering commitment to her art and principles. Her legacy as an Afro-Cuban music icon and political activist continues to inspire generations of artists and activists alike, making her an enduring symbol of strength and defiance.

Celia's Career in the US

Celia Cruz's career in the United States marked a significant turning point in her life and musical journey. After leaving Cuba in 1960 following the rise of Fidel Castro's regime, Celia found herself in a new country, faced with the challenge of starting over and establishing herself as an artist in a foreign land.

Despite the obstacles she encountered, Celia's talent and determination propelled her to new heights. She quickly gained recognition as the "Queen of Salsa" and became an emblematic figure in Afro-Cuban music. Through her powerful voice and electrifying performances, she captivated audiences and broke down barriers, transcending language and cultural differences.

Celia's refusal to sing for Fidel Castro became a defining moment in her career and a testament to her unwavering commitment to her principles. As a political activist, she used her platform to voice her opposition to the Cuban regime and advocate for freedom and democracy. Her bold stance against Castro solidified her status as a symbol of resistance and earned her the respect of many.

Furthermore, Celia's influence extended beyond the realms of politics and activism. She played a pivotal role in the rise of Latin American female singers, paving the way for future generations of divas. Her charismatic stage presence and empowering lyrics inspired countless women to pursue their dreams and break through the male-dominated music industry.

As an Afro-Latina artist, Celia embraced her cultural heritage and incorporated it into her music and activism. Her Afro-Cuban roots were evident in her vibrant rhythms and spirited performances, which showcased the rich tapestry of Afro-Caribbean influences. Celia's Afro-Latina identity was a source of pride and strength, serving as a reminder of the resilience and beauty of her heritage.

Celia's experiences as a Cuban exile greatly influenced her artistic expressions. The pain of leaving her homeland and the longing for her roots permeated her music, creating a profound connection between her and her audience. Through her songs, she expressed the struggles and triumphs of the Cuban exile experience, becoming a voice for those who had been silenced.

Celia's legacy and impact continue to resonate today. Her music transcends time and borders, inspiring generations of artists and fans alike. Her defiant voice and unwavering commitment to her principles serve as a reminder of the power of music as a form of cultural resistance. Celia Cruz's career in the United States was a testament to her extraordinary talent, indomitable spirit, and enduring legacy in the Afro-Cuban music scene and beyond.

Celia's Refusal to Sing for Fidel Castro

In the tumultuous political landscape of Cuba during the reign of Fidel Castro, one voice stood defiantly against the regime - that of Celia Cruz. Known as the Queen of Salsa, Celia Cruz was a force to be reckoned with, both on and off the stage. Her refusal to sing for Fidel Castro became a defining moment in her career, showcasing her unwavering commitment to her principles.

Celia Cruz, born in Havana in 1925, rose to fame as one of the most influential Afro-Cuban singers of her time. With her powerful voice and vibrant stage presence, she captivated audiences around the world. However, it was her refusal to perform for Castro that truly cemented her status as a political activist.

During the early years of Castro's regime, he sought to use the power of music and art to promote his socialist agenda. As a beloved icon in the Afro-Cuban music scene, Celia Cruz was a natural choice to be part of these propaganda efforts. However, she saw through Castro's facade and recognized the oppressive nature of his regime.

Celia's refusal to sing for Castro was a bold act of defiance. It sent a clear message that she would not be silenced or co-opted by a dictator. Her decision was met with backlash from the Cuban government, who attempted to tarnish her reputation and suppress her music. But Celia remained steadfast in her beliefs, continuing to use her voice to speak out against injustice.

Beyond her refusal to perform for Castro, Celia Cruz's activism extended beyond the political realm. She used her platform to advocate for the rights of Afro-Latinos and women in the music industry. She championed cultural resistance, celebrating her African heritage and embracing her Afro-Latina identity.

Celia Cruz's refusal to sing for Fidel Castro was a defining moment in her career and a testament to her unwavering principles. Her actions demonstrated the power of music as a form of resistance and the importance of using one's platform to speak out against injustice. Her legacy continues to inspire musicians, activists, and fans around the world, reminding us of the enduring impact of her defiant voice.

Impact of Celia's Decision on her Career and Reputation

Celia Cruz, the legendary Afro-Cuban singer, made a bold decision that would forever shape her career and reputation. In the face of political pressure, she refused to sing for dictator Fidel Castro, a move that would have profound consequences.

Cruz's decision had a significant impact on her career. By standing up against the Cuban regime, she became a symbol of resistance and a voice for the Cuban exile community. This decision not only solidified her place in history but also propelled her to international fame. Cruz's refusal to compromise her beliefs allowed her to gain a loyal following who admired her for her integrity and defiance.

Furthermore, her decision helped to establish her as a political activist. Cruz used her platform to advocate for freedom and democracy, becoming an influential figure within the Cuban exile community. Her refusal to perform for Castro was not just an act of personal integrity but also a statement against the repressive Cuban regime.

Cruz's career and reputation were also shaped by her Afro-Latina identity. As an Afro-Cuban woman, she faced unique challenges in the music industry. However, she embraced her heritage and incorporated Afro-Caribbean influences into her music, creating a distinctive style that resonated with audiences worldwide. Her Afro-Latina identity became a source of empowerment and inspiration for many, as she broke down barriers and paved the way for future generations of artists.

Moreover, Cruz's decision to refuse Castro's invitation to perform was an act of cultural resistance. It was a powerful statement against the Cuban regime's suppression of artistic expression and a testament to the importance of music as a form of resistance. Her refusal demonstrated that artists have the power to challenge authority and shape the course of history.

In conclusion, Celia Cruz's decision to refuse to sing for Fidel Castro had a profound impact on her career and reputation. It solidified her place as an icon of resistance and propelled her to international fame. Her Afro-Latina identity and commitment to cultural resistance further shaped her legacy, inspiring future generations of artists and activists. Celia Cruz will forever be remembered as a defiant voice in Afro-Cuban music and a symbol of strength and integrity.

Chapter 2: Afro-Cuban Music: Exploring the Impact of Afro-Cuban Music on Celia Cruz's Career and her Contributions to the Genre

Origins of Afro-Cuban Music

The origins of Afro-Cuban music can be traced back to the transatlantic slave trade, which brought millions of Africans to the shores of Cuba. These African slaves brought with them their rich musical traditions, rhythms, and instruments, which melded with the European influences already present in Cuba to create a unique and vibrant musical genre.

The fusion of African and European musical styles gave birth to genres such as rumba, son, and mambo, which became the foundation of Afro-Cuban music. These genres were characterized by their infectious rhythms, syncopated beats, and lively melodies. They provided a voice for the Afro-Cuban community, allowing them to express their struggles, joys, and cultural identity through music.

Celia Cruz, the iconic Afro-Cuban singer, played a crucial role in popularizing Afro-Cuban music on a global scale. Born and raised in Havana, Cuba, Cruz was deeply influenced by the rhythms and melodies of Afro-Cuban music from an early age. Her powerful voice and dynamic stage presence captivated audiences, and she became known as the "Queen of Salsa" for her mastery of the genre.

Cruz's career was marked by a refusal to perform for Fidel Castro's regime, a decision that showcased her political activism and defiance. Despite facing backlash and exile, Cruz continued to use her music as a tool for cultural resistance and as a voice for the Cuban people.

Her refusal to compromise her beliefs and sing for the dictator cemented her status as a symbol of resistance and earned her the respect and admiration of many. Cruz's influence extended beyond the Afro-Cuban music scene, as she paved the way for other Latin American female singers and challenged the traditional roles of women in the music industry.

As a Afro-Latina artist, Cruz embraced her identity and celebrated her African roots in her music and activism. She shattered stereotypes and became an inspiration for Afro-Latina women around the world, challenging societal norms and advocating for equality and representation.

Cruz's legacy lives on, as her impact on the Afro-Cuban music scene and beyond cannot be overstated. Her vibrant personality, powerful voice, and unwavering dedication to her craft continue to inspire generations of musicians and fans worldwide. She remains a symbol of strength, resilience, and cultural pride, forever etching her name in the annals of Afro-Cuban music history.

Celia's Early Influences and Musical Style

Celia Cruz, known as the Defiant Voice of Afro-Cuban Music, was a musical icon who captivated audiences around the world with her powerful voice and vibrant performances. Her early influences and unique musical style played a significant role in shaping her career and establishing her as a trailblazer in the music industry.

Growing up in Havana, Cuba, Celia was exposed to a diverse range of musical genres, including Afro-Cuban rhythms, son, rumba, and bolero. These rich musical traditions laid the foundation for her future success and allowed her to develop a deep appreciation for her Afro-Caribbean heritage.

From a young age, Celia's talent and passion for singing were evident. She was heavily influenced by artists such as La Sonora Matancera, a renowned Cuban orchestra, and admired vocalists like Bola de Nieve and Paulina Alvarez. These early influences shaped her vocal style and inspired her to pursue a career in music.

Celia's musical style was characterized by her powerful voice, infectious energy, and undeniable charisma. Her performances were a fusion of Afro-Cuban rhythms, salsa, and Latin jazz, creating a unique sound that resonated with people from all walks of life. Her ability to infuse traditional Cuban music with contemporary elements made her a pioneer in the genre and opened doors for future generations of Afro-Cuban artists.

Throughout her career, Celia remained committed to preserving and promoting Afro-Cuban music. She believed in the power of music as a tool for cultural expression and resistance. Her refusal to sing for dictator Fidel Castro was a bold stand against the Cuban regime and a testament to her unwavering principles.

Celia's musical style and activism went hand in hand, as her songs often carried powerful messages of freedom, love, and unity. She used her platform to shed light on the struggles of the Afro-Latina community and to advocate for social change. Her music became a symbol of resilience, inspiring generations of artists to embrace their heritage and fight for their rights.

Celia Cruz's early influences and musical style were the driving forces behind her legendary career. Her Afro-Cuban roots, combined with her unparalleled talent and unwavering passion, allowed her to make an indelible mark on the music world. Her legacy continues to inspire and uplift, reminding us of the transformative power of music and the importance of staying true to oneself.

Collaboration with Tito Puente and Other Afro-Cuban Artists

Celia Cruz, the iconic Afro-Cuban singer, is known not only for her powerful voice and vibrant stage presence but also for her collaborations with legendary musicians. One of the most significant partnerships in her career was with the renowned percussionist and bandleader, Tito Puente, and other Afro-Cuban artists.

Cruz and Puente first joined forces in the late 1960s, creating a musical fusion that would revolutionize the Afro-Cuban music scene. Their collaboration gave birth to a new genre called "salsa," which combined traditional Cuban rhythms with elements of jazz, soul, and rock. This unique blend of sounds paved the way for a new era in Latin music, captivating audiences around the world.

Their partnership produced numerous chart-topping hits, including "Quimbara," "Bemba Colora," and "Pachito E'che." These songs not only showcased Cruz's powerful vocals but also highlighted Puente's masterful percussion skills. Together, they created a sound that was infectious, energetic, and impossible to resist.

In addition to Tito Puente, Cruz collaborated with other Afro-Cuban artists, such as Cachao, La Sonora Matancera, and Johnny Pacheco. These collaborations allowed Cruz to further explore the rich tapestry of Afro-Cuban music, incorporating diverse rhythms and melodies into her repertoire.

Cruz's collaborations with these artists went beyond the realm of music. They were a celebration of Afro-Cuban culture and a way to honor their shared heritage. Through their music, they sought to preserve and promote the vibrant traditions of their ancestors, paying homage to the African roots that shaped their artistry.

These collaborations not only propelled Cruz to international fame but also solidified her status as the voice of Afro-Cuban music. Her powerful presence and infectious energy on stage, combined with the virtuosity of her collaborators, captivated audiences worldwide and left an indelible mark on the music industry.

Celia Cruz's collaborations with Tito Puente and other Afro-Cuban artists not only enriched her own musical journey but also contributed to the evolution of Afro-Cuban music itself. Their fusion of styles and influences created a lasting legacy that continues to inspire musicians and fans alike.

In the next chapters, we will delve into other aspects of Celia Cruz's life and career, exploring her refusal to sing for Fidel Castro, her role as a political activist, and her impact on the rise of Latin American female singers. We will also discuss her experiences as a Cuban exile, her Afro-Latina identity, and the challenges faced by women in the music industry. Join us on this journey as we unravel the remarkable story of Celia Cruz, the defiant voice of Afro-Cuban music.

Popularizing Afro-Cuban Music in the United States

One of the most significant contributions that Celia Cruz made to the world of music was the popularization of Afro-Cuban music in the United States. Born and raised in Havana, Cuba, Cruz was deeply influenced by the rich and vibrant Afro-Cuban music tradition that surrounded her from a young age. As she embarked on her career as a singer, Cruz sought to share the beauty and power of Afro-Cuban music with audiences around the world, and especially in the United States.

In the mid-20th century, Afro-Cuban music was relatively unknown to mainstream American audiences. However, with her electrifying performances and unique style, Cruz managed to captivate and engage listeners, opening their eyes and ears to the beauty and complexity of Afro-Cuban rhythms.

Cruz's music blended elements of traditional Afro-Cuban genres such as son, rumba, and guaracha with modern influences, creating a sound that was both familiar and innovative. Her infectious energy and powerful voice drew people in, and soon, Afro-Cuban music began to gain popularity in the United States.

Through her collaborations with American musicians and her performances in popular venues such as The Palladium in New York City, Cruz helped to bring Afro-Cuban music into the mainstream. She became a beloved figure in the Latin music scene and gained a dedicated fan base that transcended cultural boundaries.

Cruz's success in popularizing Afro-Cuban music in the United States had a profound impact on the genre and its perception. She paved the way for future generations of Afro-Cuban musicians to find success and recognition in the American music industry. Today, Afro-Cuban music has become a staple in Latin music, and its influence can be heard in various genres such as salsa, jazz, and pop.

Celia Cruz's efforts to popularize Afro-Cuban music in the United States not only contributed to the growth and evolution of the genre but also served as a form of cultural resistance. At a time when the Cuban regime was suppressing artistic expression, Cruz's refusal to perform for Fidel Castro became an act of defiance and a symbol of freedom. Her music and activism continue to inspire and empower people around the world, making her a true icon of Afro-Cuban music and a trailblazer for future generations of artists.

Celia's Signature Sound and Impact on the Genre

Celia Cruz, the iconic Afro-Cuban singer, possessed a signature sound that revolutionized the genre and left an indelible mark on the music industry. Her powerful voice, electrifying stage presence, and infectious energy captivated audiences around the world. In this subchapter, we will explore the unique elements of Celia's sound and her lasting impact on Afro-Cuban music.

Celia's voice was a force of nature, effortlessly spanning multiple octaves and conveying a range of emotions. Her rich, vibrant timbre had an unmistakable quality that set her apart from her contemporaries. Whether she was belting out impassioned boleros or infusing her music with the infectious rhythms of salsa, Celia's voice was instantly recognizable.

But it wasn't just her voice that made Celia Cruz a legendary figure in the genre. Her ability to infuse her music with elements of Afro-Cuban culture and her unwavering commitment to preserving her heritage made her a trailblazer in the industry. She fearlessly incorporated traditional African rhythms, such as the conga and the rumba, into her songs, creating a fusion of Afro-Cuban and Latin sounds that was both innovative and deeply authentic.

Celia's impact on the genre extended far beyond her music. Her refusal to sing for dictator Fidel Castro demonstrated her unwavering commitment to her principles and made her a symbol of political activism. Her defiance against the Cuban regime was a powerful act of cultural resistance, inspiring others to stand up against oppression. Moreover, Celia's Afro-Latina identity played a significant role in her music and activism, challenging societal norms and empowering Afro-Latinas around the world.

Celia Cruz's influence on Latin American divas cannot be overstated. Her rise to stardom paved the way for countless female artists, breaking barriers and redefining the role of women in the music industry. Her larger-than-life persona and unapologetic self-expression set the stage for the diva culture that continues to thrive today.

As a Cuban exile, Celia's experiences and the experiences of other exiles profoundly influenced her artistic expressions. Her music became a reflection of the pain, resilience, and hope of a community torn apart by political turmoil. Through her lyrics and performances, she became the voice of a generation, giving voice to the struggles and triumphs of the Cuban diaspora.

Celia Cruz's legacy and impact continue to resonate. Her music transcends borders and generations, inspiring new artists to embrace their heritage and push the boundaries of their art. She remains an icon of Afro-Cuban music, forever etched in the annals of musical history. In the following chapters, we will delve deeper into the various aspects of Celia's life and career, exploring the interplay between her music, activism, and cultural identity.

Chapter 3: Political Activism: Analyzing Celia Cruz's Refusal to Sing for Fidel Castro and Exploring her Role as a Political Activist

Political Climate in Cuba and Celia's Stand against Dictatorship

In the subchapter "Political Climate in Cuba and Celia's Stand against Dictatorship," we delve into the turbulent political environment in Cuba during the rise of Fidel Castro and Celia Cruz's courageous refusal to perform for the dictator. This chapter explores the intersection of politics and music, shedding light on Celia's unwavering commitment to her principles and her role as a political activist.

Throughout the 20th century, Cuba experienced significant political upheaval, with the rise of Fidel Castro's communist regime in 1959 being a pivotal moment in the nation's history. As Castro consolidated his power, he sought to control all aspects of Cuban life, including the arts and entertainment industry. Artists were expected to align themselves with the regime and use their platforms to spread the communist ideology.

However, Celia Cruz, an iconic Afro-Cuban singer, refused to conform to these expectations. She staunchly opposed the dictator and his oppressive regime, using her music as a form of resistance. Celia's refusal to perform for Fidel Castro was a bold statement against the dictatorship and a testament to her unwavering commitment to her beliefs.

Celia's stand against dictatorship not only showcased her bravery but also highlighted the power of music as a means of political activism. Through her refusal to sing for Castro, Celia sent a powerful message to the Cuban people and the world, standing up for freedom of expression and human rights.

This subchapter also explores the broader implications of Celia's political activism. We examine her influence on the rise of Latin American female singers and her impact on the diva culture. Additionally, we delve into the experiences of Cuban exiles, including Celia Cruz, and the profound impact of their forced migration on their artistic expressions.

Furthermore, we discuss Celia's Afro-Latina identity and its significance in her music and activism. As an Afro-Cuban woman, Celia faced unique challenges in the music industry, and her success served as an inspiration to aspiring female artists. We explore the obstacles faced by women in the music industry and how Celia's career serves as a testament to their resilience and determination.

In summary, this subchapter delves into the political climate in Cuba and Celia Cruz's courageous stand against dictatorship. It explores the impact of her activism on the Afro-Cuban music scene, her influence on Latin American divas, and her role in cultural resistance. Celia's legacy as a defiant voice in Afro-Cuban music continues to inspire generations and serves as a reminder of the power of music in shaping political and social change.

Celia's Role in the Cuban Exile Community

Celia Cruz, known as the "Queen of Salsa," played a significant role in the Cuban exile community during a pivotal time in history. Born in Havana, Cuba, in 1925, Celia's vibrant voice and dynamic stage presence propelled her to international fame. However, her refusal to sing for dictator Fidel Castro in the early 1960s forever changed the trajectory of her career and solidified her place as a symbol of defiance and resistance.

As Castro's regime tightened its grip on Cuba, many artists and intellectuals felt the pressure to conform to the government's ideologies.

However, Celia Cruz stood firm in her beliefs and refused to lend her voice to a regime she believed was oppressive. This act of defiance not only showcased her unwavering commitment to her principles but also marked the beginning of her role as a political activist.

Celia's refusal to perform for Castro catapulted her into the heart of the Cuban exile community. She became a beacon of hope for those who had been forced to leave their homeland and a symbol of resistance against the oppressive regime. Through her music and activism, Celia became a voice for the voiceless, using her platform to shed light on the struggles and hardships faced by the Cuban exile community.

In addition to being a political activist, Celia Cruz's impact on the Afro-Cuban music genre cannot be overstated. Her dynamic fusion of Afro-Cuban rhythms, such as rumba and son, with elements of jazz and salsa revolutionized the music scene. Her powerful voice and infectious energy electrified audiences around the world, and she became an icon of Afro-Cuban music.

Celia's role as a cultural ambassador for the Cuban exile community extended beyond her music. Her Afro-Latina identity was a source of pride and empowerment, and she used her platform to celebrate her heritage. By embracing her African roots and incorporating them into her music and image, Celia became an inspiration for Afro-Latinas everywhere, challenging societal norms and breaking down barriers.

Today, Celia Cruz's legacy lives on. Her refusal to perform for Fidel Castro and her unwavering commitment to her principles continue to inspire artists and activists alike. Her impact on the Afro-Cuban music scene and the broader music industry is undeniable. She paved the way for future generations of Latin American female singers, leaving behind a legacy of empowerment, resilience, and cultural pride.

In conclusion, Celia Cruz's role in the Cuban exile community was multifaceted. As a political activist, she used her platform to shed light on the struggles faced by the Cuban exile community and became a symbol of resistance against the oppressive regime. As an Afro-Cuban musician, she revolutionized the music scene, blending Afro-Cuban rhythms with other genres to create a unique sound. Her Afro-Latina identity and pride in her heritage continue to inspire and empower women of color in the music industry and beyond. Celia Cruz's legacy and impact will forever be remembered as a testament to her defiance, resilience, and unwavering commitment to her principles.

Activism through Music and Public Statements

Celia Cruz: The Defiant Voice of Afro-Cuban Music

Celia Cruz was not just a legendary singer; she was also a powerful activist who used her music and public statements to fight for what she believed in. Throughout her career, she fearlessly stood up against political oppression, championed the rights of Afro-Latinos, and became a symbol of resistance and cultural pride. This subchapter explores the intersection of music and activism in Celia Cruz's life, highlighting her refusal to sing for dictator Fidel Castro and her broader role as a political activist.

Celia Cruz's refusal to perform for Fidel Castro was a defining moment in her career. Despite pressure and threats from the Cuban regime, she stood her ground and chose not to compromise her principles. This act of defiance not only solidified her reputation as a fearless artist but also made her a symbol of resistance against the oppressive regime. Her refusal to sing for Castro became a powerful statement that resonated with millions of people, both in Cuba and beyond.

But Celia Cruz's activism did not stop there. Throughout her life, she used her music as a platform to speak out against various social and political issues. Her songs often carried messages of empowerment, cultural pride, and the celebration of Afro-Cuban heritage. By using her music to address these issues, she became a powerful advocate for change and a voice for the marginalized.

Moreover, Celia Cruz's activism extended beyond her music. She was actively involved in various humanitarian causes, including supporting organizations that fought for civil rights and social justice. She used her influence to raise awareness about important issues, such as racial inequality and the rights of women in the music industry. Through her public statements and interviews, she challenged societal norms and paved the way for future generations of female artists.

Celia Cruz's activism through music and public statements had a profound impact on the Afro-Cuban music scene and beyond. Her refusal to perform for Fidel Castro was an act of cultural resistance that inspired countless others to stand up against oppression. Her music and activism continue to resonate with audiences today, reminding us of the power of music to effect social change.

In conclusion, Celia Cruz's activism through music and public statements was a testament to her courage, resilience, and unwavering commitment to her beliefs. By refusing to sing for Fidel Castro and using her music as a vehicle for social change, she became a powerful force for activism and a symbol of defiance. Her legacy as a trailblazer in the Afro-Cuban music scene and her impact on various social and political issues continue to inspire and resonate with audiences around the world.

Repercussions and Criticisms of Celia's Activism

Celia Cruz, the iconic Afro-Cuban singer, was not only known for her powerful voice and vibrant performances but also for her unwavering political activism. Throughout her career, Celia's refusal to sing for the dictator Fidel Castro and her outspoken criticism of the Cuban regime had significant repercussions, both positive and negative.

One of the most immediate consequences of Celia's activism was her exile from her beloved Cuba. As a result of her refusal to support Castro's oppressive regime, Celia was forced to leave her homeland, leaving behind her family, friends, and the country that had shaped her music. This exile experience deeply influenced her artistic expressions, as she channeled her pain and longing into her music, becoming the voice of the Cuban diaspora.

However, Celia's activism also attracted criticism and backlash from various quarters. Some argued that her refusal to perform for Castro was a betrayal of her Cuban heritage and accused her of being a traitor. Others believed that she should have used her platform to promote unity and diplomacy rather than engaging in political activism. Despite these criticisms, Celia remained steadfast in her beliefs, using her voice to shed light on the injustices faced by the Cuban people.

Furthermore, Celia's activism also had a significant impact on her career and the music industry as a whole. While her refusal to perform for Castro may have led to the loss of opportunities in Cuba, it opened doors for her internationally. Celia's defiant stance against the Cuban regime garnered her immense support and admiration from fans around the world who saw her as a symbol of resistance and freedom.

Celia Cruz's activism also paved the way for other Latin American female singers, inspiring them to use their platforms for social and political causes. Her influence on the rise of Latin American divas and the diva culture cannot be overstated. Celia's unwavering commitment to her principles set a precedent for future generations of artists, encouraging them to speak out against oppression and injustice.

In conclusion, Celia Cruz's activism had far-reaching repercussions and attracted both praise and criticism. Her refusal to sing for Fidel Castro and her outspoken criticism of the Cuban regime led to her exile and loss of opportunities in her homeland. However, her activism also propelled her to international stardom and inspired a generation of artists to use their voices for social and political change. Celia Cruz's legacy as a defiant voice of Afro-Cuban music and a symbol of resistance continues to resonate and inspire to this day.

Legacy of Celia's Political Activism

Celia Cruz, the legendary Afro-Cuban singer, is not only known for her remarkable voice and vibrant performances but also for her unwavering political stance. Throughout her career, Cruz used her platform to advocate for social justice and actively resist oppressive regimes. In this subchapter, we delve into the lasting legacy of Celia's political activism and explore the impact it had on various aspects of society.

Celia Cruz's refusal to sing for Fidel Castro stands as a defining moment in her career. By making this bold decision, she demonstrated her commitment to her principles and her refusal to compromise her beliefs for personal gain. Cruz's stance against the Cuban dictatorship resonated with audiences around the world, especially those who had experienced the oppressive regime firsthand. Her act of defiance became a symbol of resistance, inspiring others to stand up against injustice.

Furthermore, Celia's political activism played a crucial role in shaping the Afro-Cuban music genre. Her refusal to perform for Castro brought attention to the struggles faced by Afro-Cuban musicians and artists under his regime. By speaking out against the government, she opened doors for other artists to express themselves freely and paved the way for the Afro-Cuban music scene to flourish.

Celia Cruz's influence extended beyond her music and activism, as she became a trailblazer for Latin American female singers. Her powerful voice, vibrant stage presence, and unapologetic personality challenged traditional gender norms and established her as a symbol of female empowerment. Through her success, she shattered glass ceilings and inspired a new generation of Latin American divas who followed in her footsteps.

As a Cuban exile, Celia Cruz's experiences and struggles as a migrant artist shaped her artistic expressions. She channeled her pain, longing, and resilience into her music, creating a unique blend of Afro-Cuban rhythms and Caribbean influences. Her migration journey became a source of inspiration for her lyrics, resonating with others who shared similar experiences of displacement and longing for their homeland.

Celia Cruz's Afro-Latina identity played a significant role in her music and activism. As a woman of African descent in a predominantly white industry, she faced numerous challenges and discrimination. However, she embraced her heritage and used her platform to celebrate Afro-Latina culture, challenging stereotypes and promoting cultural diversity.

The legacy of Celia Cruz is not limited to her music and activism but extends to her impact on the music industry as a whole. Her refusal to perform for Fidel Castro was not just an act of defiance; it was a powerful act of cultural resistance. Cruz's bold stance showcased the power of music as a tool for political change and inspired generations of artists to use their voices to challenge oppressive systems.

In conclusion, Celia Cruz's political activism left a lasting legacy that transcended the realms of music and politics. Her refusal to sing for Fidel Castro, her role in empowering women in music, her celebration of Afro-Latina identity, and her impact on the Afro-Cuban music scene are just a few aspects of her multifaceted legacy. Celia Cruz's unwavering commitment to her principles and her fearless pursuit of social justice continue to inspire and resonate with audiences around the world. Her legacy serves as a reminder of the power of music to effect change and the importance of using one's platform for the greater good.

Chapter 4: Latin American Divas: Examining Celia Cruz's Influence on the Rise of Latin American Female Singers and her Impact on the Diva Culture

The Emergence of Latin American Divas

Latin American music has seen the emergence of many talented and influential female singers, but few have left a mark as indelible as Celia Cruz. Born and raised in Havana, Cuba, Cruz's journey from a struggling young singer to one of the most celebrated Latin American divas is a testament to her undeniable talent, resilience, and unwavering spirit.

Cruz's rise to stardom can be traced back to the impact of Afro-Cuban music on her career. Drawing inspiration from the rich musical traditions of her Afro-Cuban heritage, Cruz infused her music with infectious rhythms and soulful melodies that captivated audiences worldwide. Her unique blend of Afro-Cuban sounds, such as son, rumba, and guaracha, helped define a new era in Latin American music, setting the stage for the emergence of other Latin American divas.

One of the defining moments in Cruz's career was her refusal to sing for Fidel Castro, the notorious Cuban dictator. This act of defiance not only showcased Cruz's unwavering commitment to her principles but also solidified her role as a political activist. By using her platform to speak out against the Cuban regime, Cruz became a symbol of resistance, inspiring other artists to use their voice for social and political change.

Cruz's influence on the rise of Latin American female singers cannot be overstated. Through her groundbreaking performances and empowering lyrics, she shattered stereotypes and paved the way for future generations of divas. Her unapologetic embrace of her Afro-Latina identity resonated with audiences worldwide, challenging societal norms and celebrating cultural diversity.

As a Cuban exile, Cruz's experiences shaped her artistic expressions. The pain of leaving her homeland and starting anew in the United States infused her music with a profound sense of longing and resilience. Through her songs, she captured the essence of the Cuban exile experience, providing a voice for those who were forced to leave their homes and rebuild their lives in a foreign land.

Cruz's legacy extends far beyond her music. Her refusal to perform for Fidel Castro was more than just an act of defiance; it was a powerful form of cultural resistance. By rejecting the Cuban regime, Cruz demonstrated the power of music as a tool for social change, inspiring others to challenge oppressive systems and fight for justice.

In conclusion, Celia Cruz's emergence as a Latin American diva was a result of her undeniable talent, cultural pride, and unwavering commitment to her principles. Through her music, she not only revolutionized the Latin American music scene but also inspired a new generation of artists to use their voice for social and political change. Her legacy as a trailblazer, activist, and cultural icon continues to resonate with audiences worldwide, cementing her status as one of the greatest Latin American divas of all time.

Celia's Unique Style and Stage Presence

Celia Cruz was not just a singer; she was a force to be reckoned with on the stage. Her unique style and stage presence captivated audiences around the world and solidified her status as the Queen of Salsa.

From the moment she stepped onto the stage, Celia commanded attention. Her vibrant and colorful costumes, adorned with feathers, sequins, and ruffles, reflected her larger-than-life personality. Celia's wardrobe choices were an extension of her music, representing the joy, energy, and passion that she brought to her performances.

But it wasn't just her wardrobe that made Celia stand out. It was her electrifying stage presence. With every step, every movement, every note, she radiated energy that was infectious. Celia's performances were a masterclass in showmanship, as she effortlessly danced, twirled, and interacted with her band and the audience. She had an uncanny ability to connect with her audience on a deep emotional level, making everyone in the crowd feel like they were a part of something special.

Celia's unique style and stage presence were also a reflection of her Afro-Cuban roots. She drew inspiration from the Afro-Caribbean musical traditions, infusing her music with the rhythms of salsa, son, rumba, and guaguancó. Her powerful voice, with its distinctive vibrato and melodic improvisation, was the perfect vehicle for expressing the soul and spirit of Afro-Cuban music.

But Celia's stage presence was more than just a performance; it was an act of defiance. She used her platform to speak out against the injustices and political oppression that plagued her homeland of Cuba. Celia's refusal to sing for Fidel Castro was not just a personal decision; it was a statement of solidarity with the Cuban people and a rejection of the authoritarian regime.

Celia's unique style and stage presence had a lasting impact on the world of music. She paved the way for a new generation of Latin American female singers, inspiring them to embrace their own unique identities and styles. Her legacy continues to resonate today, as her influence can be heard in the voices of artists like Gloria Estefan, Jennifer Lopez, and Shakira.

In conclusion, Celia Cruz's unique style and stage presence were more than just a performance; they were a reflection of her Afro-Cuban roots, a statement of defiance, and an inspiration to future generations of musicians. Her legacy as the Queen of Salsa lives on, forever etched in the hearts of those who were fortunate enough to witness her electrifying performances.

Breaking Barriers for Women in the Music Industry

In the male-dominated world of the music industry, women have long faced numerous challenges and barriers. However, there are trailblazers like Celia Cruz who have defied the odds and shattered glass ceilings, leaving an indelible mark on the industry. In this subchapter, we delve into the remarkable journey of Celia Cruz and her role in breaking barriers for women in the music industry.

Celia Cruz, the defiant voice of Afro-Cuban music, faced multiple obstacles throughout her career. As a woman of color in a predominantly white industry, she encountered discrimination, marginalization, and the pervasive gender stereotypes of her time. However, her sheer talent, determination, and refusal to conform propelled her to unprecedented heights.

Cruz's Afro-Cuban music was a revolutionary force that transcended boundaries, captivating audiences worldwide. Her music reflected the impact of her Afro-Cuban roots, blending traditional rhythms with contemporary sounds. Through her powerful voice and electrifying performances, she challenged societal norms and redefined the possibilities for women in music.

Cruz's refusal to sing for Fidel Castro showcased her unwavering commitment to her principles and her role as a political activist. This act of defiance not only solidified her status as an icon but also became a symbol of cultural resistance against the Cuban regime. By taking a stand, she empowered countless women to find their voices and use them to effect change.

The influence of Celia Cruz extended beyond her music, as she paved the way for a new generation of Latin American divas. Her unapologetic presence, fierce stage persona, and larger-than-life diva culture left an indelible impact on the music industry. She inspired women to embrace their power, embrace their artistry, and challenge societal expectations.

As a Cuban exile, Cruz's experiences and the experiences of other Cuban exiles significantly influenced her artistic expressions. Through her music, she channeled the pain, longing, and resilience of those forced to leave their homeland. Her songs became anthems for the dispossessed, giving voice to the struggles and hopes of a displaced community.

Cruz's Afro-Latina identity was a central theme in her music and activism. By embracing her heritage, she celebrated the richness and diversity of Afro-Latin culture. Her music became a platform to challenge racial stereotypes, promote cultural pride, and unite people from different backgrounds.

Celia Cruz's career also shed light on the challenges faced by women in the music industry. Through her personal struggles and triumphs, she exposed the gender disparities, unequal opportunities, and systemic biases that hinder women's progress. Her success paved the way for future generations to demand equality and reshape the industry.

In conclusion, Celia Cruz's journey serves as a testament to the power of perseverance, talent, and courage. Through her refusal to conform, she broke barriers, challenged societal norms, and left an enduring legacy. Her impact on the Afro-Cuban music scene and beyond is immeasurable, inspiring women to embrace their voices, celebrate their heritage, and defy the odds in pursuit of their dreams.

Celia's Influence on Future Latin American Divas

Celia Cruz's Influence on Future Latin American Divas

Celia Cruz, known as the "Defiant Voice of Afro-Cuban Music," left an indelible mark on the music industry and, in particular, on the rise of Latin American divas. Her unique style, powerful voice, and unwavering determination continue to inspire female artists across Latin America to this day.

As an Afro-Cuban artist, Celia Cruz faced numerous challenges in a predominantly male and racially biased industry. However, her refusal to be silenced and her commitment to her craft transformed her into a symbol of strength and resilience for all women in music. By breaking through barriers and defying societal expectations, she paved the way for future Latin American divas to follow their dreams and assert their voices.

Celia Cruz's influence on the diva culture can be seen in the way she embraced her own identity and celebrated her Afro-Latina heritage. She fearlessly incorporated Afro-Caribbean rhythms and traditions into her music, creating a sound that was uniquely her own. This fusion of genres and cultures became a blueprint for other Latin American female artists who sought to express their own experiences and cultural backgrounds through their music.

Furthermore, Celia Cruz's refusal to sing for Fidel Castro and her role as a political activist resonated deeply with Latin American divas. Her decision to stand up against a dictator demonstrated her unwavering commitment to her principles and the power of using music as a tool for social change. This activism inspired many future artists to use their platforms to advocate for justice and equality.

Celia Cruz's impact on Latin American divas goes beyond her music and activism. Her status as a Cuban exile and her experiences as a migrant artist added another layer of complexity to her identity. Through her art, she shared the stories and struggles of Cuban exiles, shedding light on the harsh realities faced by those who were forced to leave their homeland. This exploration of the Cuban exile experience resonated with other Latin American artists who had experienced displacement and migration, allowing them to connect with their own roots and share their own narratives through their music.

In conclusion, Celia Cruz's influence on future Latin American divas cannot be overstated. Her defiance, resilience, and commitment to her craft continue to inspire female artists across the region. Through her music, activism, and exploration of her Afro-Latina identity, she challenged societal norms, broke barriers, and created a lasting legacy that transcends borders and generations. Celia Cruz will forever be remembered as a trailblazer who paved the way for Latin American divas to claim their rightful place in the music industry.

The Concept of Diva Culture in Latin American Music

In the vibrant world of Latin American music, the concept of diva culture has played a significant role in shaping and defining the genre. One of the most prominent figures in this culture is the legendary Celia Cruz, whose larger-than-life persona and powerful voice made her an icon in the music industry. This subchapter explores the concept of diva culture in Latin American music, with a focus on Celia Cruz and her contributions to the genre.

Celia Cruz, often referred to as the "Queen of Salsa," embodied the essence of diva culture. Her extravagant costumes, flamboyant stage presence, and commanding vocals captivated audiences around the world. Cruz's incredible talent and undeniable charisma set her apart from her contemporaries, making her a true diva in every sense of the word.

Through her music, Celia Cruz brought Afro-Cuban rhythms to the forefront of Latin American music, revolutionizing the genre and paving the way for future generations of artists. Her fusion of traditional Cuban music with elements of jazz, soul, and salsa created a unique sound that resonated with audiences of all backgrounds.

Not only did Celia Cruz revolutionize Latin American music, but she also used her platform to advocate for political change. Her refusal to perform for Fidel Castro, the dictator of Cuba, showcased her unwavering commitment to her principles and made her a symbol of resistance against oppressive regimes. Cruz's political activism further solidified her status as a diva, as she fearlessly used her voice to fight for justice and freedom.

Celia Cruz's influence extends beyond her music and activism. She played a pivotal role in the rise of Latin American female singers, breaking down barriers and challenging the male-dominated music industry. Her success inspired a new generation of divas who followed in her footsteps, empowering women to express their talents and assert their identities in a male-dominated world.

Furthermore, Celia Cruz's Afro-Latina identity was a crucial aspect of her music and activism. As an Afro-Cuban artist, she celebrated her African roots and used her platform to challenge stereotypes and promote Afro-Latinx culture. Her music became a vehicle for cultural resistance, breaking down barriers and promoting inclusivity.

In conclusion, the concept of diva culture in Latin American music is exemplified by the extraordinary career of Celia Cruz. Her talent, charisma, and activism made her an icon and a trailblazer in the genre. Cruz's legacy as a diva continues to inspire and empower artists today, cementing her status as a true legend of Afro-Cuban music.

Chapter 5: Cuban Exile Experience: Investigating the Experiences of Cuban Exiles, including Celia Cruz, and their Impact on their Artistic Expressions

The Cuban Revolution and Exile

The Cuban Revolution, led by Fidel Castro, had a profound impact on the life and career of the iconic Afro-Cuban singer, Celia Cruz. Born and raised in Havana, Cuba, Cruz rose to fame as the "Queen of Salsa" and became an international symbol of Afro-Cuban music. However, her refusal to sing for Fidel Castro marked a pivotal moment in her life and cemented her status as a political activist.

Cruz's decision to turn down the opportunity to perform for Castro was a bold statement of resistance against the Cuban regime. She believed that singing for Castro would go against her principles and the values she held dear. This act of defiance not only showcased her strong character but also solidified her role as a political activist, using her platform to speak out against an oppressive regime.

The Cuban Revolution also led to Cruz's forced exile from her beloved homeland. Like many other Cubans who opposed the Castro regime, she was forced to leave her country and start a new life elsewhere. This experience of exile profoundly influenced her artistic expressions, as she channeled her feelings of nostalgia, loss, and longing for Cuba into her music. Through her powerful vocals and emotional performances, Cruz became a voice for the Cuban diaspora, bringing their experiences to the forefront and shedding light on the struggles faced by exiled Cubans.

Cruz's Afro-Latina identity played a significant role in her music and activism. As an Afro-Cuban woman, she faced discrimination and marginalization both within and outside the music industry. However, she defied societal expectations and broke down barriers, becoming a trailblazer for women in music. Her success paved the way for other Latin American female singers, contributing to the rise of the diva culture and empowering women to take center stage in a male-dominated industry.

The legacy of Celia Cruz continues to resonate today, as her impact on Afro-Cuban music and beyond is undeniable. Her refusal to perform for Fidel Castro was not only an act of cultural resistance but also a testament to her unwavering commitment to her principles. Through her music, activism, and perseverance, Cruz left an indelible mark on the Afro-Cuban music scene and inspired generations of artists to embrace their cultural heritage and use their voices to enact change. Her legacy lives on, reminding us of the power of music to transcend borders, unite people, and ignite social change.

Challenges Faced by Cuban Exiles in the United States

The journey of Cuban exiles to the United States has been marked by numerous challenges, as they strive to rebuild their lives in a foreign land. Celia Cruz, the defiant voice of Afro-Cuban music, was no exception to these struggles. In this subchapter, we delve into the hardships faced by Cuban exiles in the United States and how they impacted Celia Cruz's artistic expressions and activism.

Forced to leave their homeland due to political upheaval and the repressive regime of Fidel Castro, Cuban exiles faced a multitude of obstacles upon their arrival in the United States. Language barriers, cultural differences, and the need to adapt to a new way of life all presented significant challenges. These difficulties were compounded by the loss of their homes, belongings, and the separation from loved ones left behind in Cuba.

Celia Cruz, like many other Cuban exiles, experienced a deep sense of longing for her home country. However, instead of allowing these challenges to consume her, she channeled her emotions into her music. Through her powerful voice and passionate performances, Cruz not only connected with other exiles who shared her experiences but also captivated audiences worldwide.

Furthermore, the Cuban exile experience greatly influenced Cruz's artistry. The pain of displacement and the longing for freedom were recurrent themes in her music, infusing it with a unique sense of resilience and defiance. Her songs became anthems for those who had been uprooted from their homeland, serving as a source of solace and inspiration.

In addition to the emotional struggles faced by Cuban exiles, they also encountered practical difficulties in establishing themselves in the United States. Limited job opportunities, financial instability, and the need to navigate a complex immigration system were constant challenges. Despite these obstacles, many Cuban exiles, including Celia Cruz, persevered and succeeded in building successful careers and making significant contributions to their new country.

The challenges faced by Cuban exiles in the United States not only shaped Celia Cruz's artistic expressions but also fueled her activism. Through her refusal to sing for Fidel Castro, Cruz became a symbol of resistance against the Cuban regime. Her actions inspired other exiles to stand up against oppression and fight for their rights.

In conclusion, the challenges faced by Cuban exiles in the United States were numerous and profound. From the emotional toll of displacement to the practical obstacles of starting anew, these struggles shaped the experiences of individuals like Celia Cruz. However, through her music and activism, Cruz overcame these challenges and left a lasting legacy that continues to inspire generations.

Celia's Personal Experiences as a Cuban Exile

In this subchapter, we delve into the personal experiences of the legendary Afro-Cuban singer, Celia Cruz, as a Cuban exile. Forced to leave her beloved homeland due to political unrest and the rise of Fidel Castro's dictatorship, Celia's exile had a profound impact on her artistic expressions and outlook on life.

Celia's journey as a Cuban exile began in 1960 when she and her husband, Pedro Knight, chose to leave their homeland and seek refuge in the United States. This decision was not easy for Celia, as she had to leave behind her family, friends, and the vibrant music scene that she had become synonymous with.

As we explore Celia's personal experiences, we gain a deeper understanding of the challenges faced by Cuban exiles during this tumultuous time. The feeling of displacement, the loss of cultural identity, and the struggle to adapt to a new country were common themes among Cuban exiles, and Celia was no exception. However, despite these hardships, Celia's indomitable spirit and passion for music fueled her determination to succeed in her new surroundings.

Through interviews, personal anecdotes, and archival materials, we gain insight into the ways in which Celia's exile influenced her artistic expressions. Her music became a vehicle for expressing her longing for her homeland, her love for her people, and her unwavering commitment to freedom and democracy. Songs like "Quimbara" and "La Vida Es Un Carnaval" became anthems for Cuban exiles, resonating with their shared experiences of struggle and resilience.

Furthermore, Celia's personal experiences as a Cuban exile also shaped her role as a political activist. Her refusal to sing for Fidel Castro became a symbol of defiance and resistance, making her an icon for those who opposed the Cuban regime. Celia's activism extended beyond her music, as she used her platform and influence to raise awareness about the plight of Cuban exiles and advocate for their rights.

In this subchapter, we not only explore Celia's personal experiences as a Cuban exile but also shed light on the larger context of the Cuban exile experience. By examining the impact of exile on Celia's artistic expressions, we gain a deeper appreciation for the resilience and strength of Cuban exiles and their contributions to the world of music and culture.

Through Celia's personal experiences, we uncover the power of music as a tool for resistance, healing, and cultural preservation. Her story serves as a testament to the indomitable human spirit and the enduring legacy of those who refuse to be silenced.

Artistic Expression as a Form of Resistance and Identity

Artistic expression has long been recognized as a powerful tool for resistance and a means of asserting one's identity. In the case of Celia Cruz, the Afro-Cuban singer who refused to sing for dictator Fidel Castro, her artistry became a form of defiance and a way to assert her Afro-Cuban identity.

Cruz, often referred to as the "Queen of Salsa," used her music to challenge the oppressive regime of Castro. Her refusal to perform for the dictator was a bold act of defiance, sending a message that she would not be complicit in the repression of her people. By using her artistic platform to resist the regime, Cruz became a symbol of hope and inspiration for many who were oppressed by the Cuban government.

Furthermore, Cruz's music was deeply rooted in her Afro-Cuban heritage. She drew inspiration from Afro-Cuban rhythms and incorporated them into her vibrant and energetic performances. Through her music, Cruz celebrated her roots and embraced her Afro-Latina identity. Her powerful voice and mesmerizing stage presence captivated audiences worldwide, making her a trailblazer for future generations of Afro-Latinx artists.

Cruz's refusal to sing for Castro also highlighted her role as a political activist. She used her fame and influence to shed light on the injustices faced by her people and to advocate for change. Her activism extended beyond her music, as she actively participated in protests and raised awareness about the struggles of the Cuban people.

In addition to her political activism, Cruz had a profound impact on the rise of Latin American female singers and the diva culture. Her success paved the way for other women in the music industry, breaking down barriers and challenging gender norms. Cruz's unapologetic confidence and powerful presence made her an icon for women in music, inspiring them to embrace their talent and assert their worth.

Cruz's experiences as a Cuban exile also played a significant role in her artistic expressions. Like many other exiles, she faced the challenges of leaving her homeland and starting anew in a foreign country. These experiences shaped her music and added depth to her performances, as she sought to preserve her Cuban identity while adapting to her new surroundings.

The legacy of Celia Cruz is undeniable. Her impact on the Afro-Cuban music scene and beyond is immeasurable. Through her artistry, she not only resisted a repressive regime but also celebrated her identity and paved the way for future generations of artists. Cruz's music will forever serve as a testament to the power of artistic expression as a form of resistance and a means of asserting one's identity.

Impact of Exile on Celia's Music and Lyrics

In the subchapter titled "Impact of Exile on Celia's Music and Lyrics," we delve into the profound influence that exile had on Celia Cruz's artistic expression, particularly her music and lyrics. Celia Cruz, the defiant voice of Afro-Cuban music, experienced firsthand the hardships and challenges faced by Cuban exiles during her forced departure from her beloved homeland.

Exile, for Celia, was not just a physical separation from her country; it was a rupture that deeply affected her sense of identity and belonging. As she navigated a new life in the United States, Celia's music became a vehicle for expressing her longing for Cuba and her determination to preserve her cultural heritage.

One of the most evident impacts of exile on Celia's music was the infusion of nostalgia and longing in her lyrics. Her songs evoked the bittersweet memories of her homeland, capturing the essence of Cuban culture and the vibrant spirit of its people. Through her powerful voice and heartfelt lyrics, Celia transported her audience to the streets of Havana, creating an emotional connection that resonated with both Cuban exiles and the general public.

Furthermore, exile fueled Celia's activism and determination to use her platform as an artist to denounce the oppressive regime of Fidel Castro. By refusing to sing for Castro, she sent a powerful message of resistance and solidarity with her fellow exiles. Celia's music became a tool of protest, a way to challenge the political status quo and give voice to the silenced.

The impact of exile on Celia's music extended beyond the lyrical content. Her time in exile also exposed her to new musical influences and collaborations, shaping her unique sound that blended Afro-Cuban rhythms with elements of jazz, salsa, and Latin pop. This fusion of genres and styles not only captivated audiences worldwide but also contributed to the evolution of Afro-Cuban music as a genre.

In conclusion, the impact of exile on Celia Cruz's music and lyrics was profound. It transformed her into a cultural icon, a symbol of resistance, and a voice for the voiceless. Through her music, Celia preserved her cultural heritage, challenged political oppression, and left a lasting legacy that continues to inspire generations of artists and activists.

Chapter 6: Afro-Latina Identity: Discussing Celia Cruz's Afro-Latina Identity and its Significance in her Music and Activism

Afro-Latina Identity in Latin American and Caribbean Contexts

The subchapter titled "Afro-Latina Identity in Latin American and Caribbean Contexts" delves into the significance of Celia Cruz's Afro-Latina identity and its profound impact on her music and activism. This chapter aims to provide an in-depth understanding of how Celia Cruz's Afro-Latina identity influenced her artistic expression and contributed to her role as a trailblazing figure in the Latin American and Caribbean music scene.

Celia Cruz, often referred to as the "Queen of Salsa," was not only an icon in the world of music but also a symbol of resistance and empowerment for Afro-Latinas. As an Afro-Cuban woman, she faced the challenges of racism and discrimination throughout her life, which she skillfully channeled into her music. Her Afro-Latina identity became a source of strength, allowing her to connect with her roots and celebrate her heritage through her art.

In this subchapter, we explore the intersectionality of Celia Cruz's identity as an Afro-Latina and the cultural richness of Latin American and Caribbean societies. We examine how her Afro-Cuban roots influenced her musical style, incorporating Afro-Caribbean influences and rhythms into her music. Additionally, we investigate the experiences of Cuban exiles, including Celia Cruz, and the impact of their displacement on their artistic expressions.

Furthermore, we analyze Celia Cruz's refusal to sing for Fidel Castro and the political activism that defined her career. By refusing to perform for the dictator, she became a symbol of resistance against the oppressive Cuban regime. We explore how her political activism and defiance were rooted in her Afro-Latina identity, advocating for justice and equality for all.

This subchapter also delves into Celia Cruz's role in paving the way for other Latin American female singers and her impact on the diva culture. Her unwavering determination and powerful voice shattered stereotypes and provided inspiration for countless women in the music industry.

Finally, we discuss the lasting legacy of Celia Cruz and her impact on the Afro-Cuban music scene and beyond. Her influence continues to resonate today, as her music and activism inspire a new generation of artists and activists. Celia Cruz's Afro-Latina identity serves as a reminder of the rich cultural tapestry of Latin America and the Caribbean and the power of music to transcend boundaries.

This subchapter aims to provide a comprehensive exploration of Celia Cruz's Afro-Latina identity within the Latin American and Caribbean contexts. Through her music and activism, she broke barriers, challenged societal norms, and left an indelible mark on the world of music and beyond.

Celia's Connection to her African Roots

Celia Cruz, the iconic Afro-Cuban singer, was deeply connected to her African roots, and this connection played a significant role in shaping both her music and her activism. Born and raised in Havana, Cuba, Celia was exposed to the vibrant Afro-Cuban culture that permeated the streets of her hometown. It was in this cultural melting pot that she discovered the rich rhythms, melodies, and traditions that would become the foundation of her musical career.

From an early age, Celia was drawn to the rhythms of African-influenced music, such as rumba and son. She found solace and inspiration in the beats that echoed the ancestral voices of her African heritage. These rhythms became the heartbeat of her music, infusing her performances with a power and energy that captivated audiences around the world.

Celia's connection to her African roots also informed her activism and political stance. She understood that the Afro-Cuban community faced discrimination and marginalization, both within Cuba and beyond its borders. Celia refused to remain silent in the face of injustice, using her voice to speak out against the oppressive regime of Fidel Castro. Her refusal to perform for Castro was not only an act of defiance but also a statement of solidarity with her fellow Afro-Cubans, whose voices were often silenced.

Through her music and activism, Celia became a symbol of resistance and empowerment for Afro-Cubans and marginalized communities everywhere. She shattered stereotypes and challenged societal norms, paving the way for future generations of artists to embrace their cultural heritage and express themselves authentically.

Celia's connection to her African roots also had a profound impact on the genre of Afro-Cuban music. Her unique blend of African rhythms, Latin melodies, and powerhouse vocals revolutionized the music scene, creating a style that was distinctly her own. She became a trailblazer for Afro-Cuban music, breaking down barriers and opening doors for other artists to explore and celebrate their cultural identity.

Today, Celia's legacy lives on, her impact reverberating through the Afro-Cuban music scene and beyond. Her refusal to be silenced and her unyielding dedication to her African roots continue to inspire artists and activists around the world. Celia Cruz will forever be remembered as the defiant voice of Afro-Cuban music, a symbol of strength, resilience, and cultural pride.

Embracing Afro-Latina Identity in Music and Fashion

Throughout her career, Celia Cruz embraced her Afro-Latina identity, both in her music and her fashion choices. As a prominent figure in the Afro-Cuban music scene, Cruz utilized her platform to celebrate and uplift her African heritage, breaking down barriers and challenging societal norms.

In her music, Cruz incorporated Afro-Cuban rhythms and African-inspired melodies, infusing her songs with the vibrant sounds of her heritage. Through her powerful voice and energetic performances, she brought Afro-Cuban music to the global stage, introducing audiences around the world to the rich cultural traditions of the African diaspora.

Cruz's fashion choices were equally as influential in embracing her Afro-Latina identity. She often adorned herself in vibrant, colorful outfits, incorporating traditional African prints and accessories. By proudly displaying her African roots through her fashion, Cruz challenged the Eurocentric beauty standards prevalent in the entertainment industry, asserting that Afro-Latinas could be both talented and beautiful.

Beyond her artistic contributions, Cruz's embrace of her Afro-Latina identity had a profound impact on various niches. In the realm of Latin American divas, she paved the way for future female artists, demonstrating that Afro-Latina women could achieve success in a predominantly male-dominated industry. Her influence on the rise of Latin American female singers and her embodiment of the diva culture made her an icon for aspiring artists.

Cruz's refusal to perform for Fidel Castro was not only a political statement but also an act of cultural resistance. By standing up against the Cuban regime, she demonstrated the power of music as a tool for social change. Her defiance inspired others to challenge oppressive systems and fight for their beliefs.

As a Cuban exile, Cruz's experiences greatly influenced her artistic expressions. The pain of leaving her homeland and the struggles of starting anew in a foreign country were reflected in her music, lending authenticity and depth to her performances. Her status as a migrant artist also highlighted the influence of migration on music, as she brought the sounds of her homeland to new audiences while incorporating elements of her new surroundings.

In conclusion, Celia Cruz's embrace of her Afro-Latina identity in music and fashion was a groundbreaking act of defiance and celebration. Through her music, she introduced the world to the vibrant rhythms of Afro-Cuban music and African traditions. Through her fashion choices, she challenged societal beauty standards and empowered Afro-Latinas to embrace their heritage. Her impact on the Afro-Cuban music scene and beyond is a testament to the power of embracing one's identity and using it as a force for change.

Impact of Celia's Afro-Latina Identity on her Activism

Subchapter Title: Impact of Celia's Afro-Latina Identity on her Activism

Celia Cruz: The Defiant Voice of Afro-Cuban Music

As a prominent figure in the world of Afro-Cuban music and a symbol of resistance, Celia Cruz's activism was deeply influenced by her Afro-Latina identity. Her unique blend of African and Latin roots not only shaped her music but also fueled her determination to fight for justice and freedom.

Celia Cruz's Afro-Latina identity played a significant role in her activism, as it connected her to the struggles of both the African and Latin American communities. By embracing her heritage, she became a powerful voice for Afro-Cubans and Afro-Latinos, challenging societal norms and advocating for their rights.

Through her refusal to sing for dictator Fidel Castro, Celia Cruz demonstrated her unwavering commitment to her principles. Her decision was not only a stand against the oppressive regime but also an act of cultural resistance. By refusing to lend her voice to a regime that oppressed her people, she used her platform to make a bold statement and raise awareness of the injustices faced by the Cuban people.

Celia Cruz's Afro-Latina identity also had a profound impact on her music. She infused her songs with Afro-Caribbean rhythms and African-inspired beats, creating a unique sound that celebrated her roots. By incorporating elements of her heritage into her music, she not only preserved Afro-Cuban traditions but also brought them to a wider audience, thus contributing to the growth and recognition of Afro-Cuban music.

Furthermore, Celia Cruz's Afro-Latina identity played a crucial role in inspiring other Latin American divas and empowering women in the music industry. Her success and refusal to conform to societal expectations shattered barriers and paved the way for future generations of female artists. She became an icon for women in music, showing them that they could be both artistically powerful and socially conscious.

In conclusion, Celia Cruz's Afro-Latina identity had a profound impact on her activism, music, and legacy. By embracing her roots and using her platform to fight for justice, she became a symbol of resistance and empowerment. Her refusal to sing for Fidel Castro and her contributions to Afro-Cuban music and culture have left an indelible mark on the world, inspiring generations to come.

Chapter 7: Women in Music: Exploring the Challenges Faced by Women in the Music Industry through the Lens of Celia Cruz's Career

Gender Inequality and Stereotypes in the Music Industry

Throughout history, the music industry has been plagued by gender inequality and stereotypes, with women often facing significant challenges and barriers to success. In the subchapter titled "Gender Inequality and Stereotypes in the Music Industry," we will explore these issues in the context of the legendary Afro-Cuban singer Celia Cruz, who defied societal expectations and became an icon in the male-dominated music industry.

Celia Cruz's journey serves as a powerful example of the struggles faced by women in music. As a woman of color, she faced multiple layers of discrimination and stereotypes. Despite these obstacles, she fearlessly pursued her passion for music, breaking through gender barriers and shattering stereotypes along the way.

One of the key aspects we will examine is the limited roles traditionally assigned to women in music. Women were often expected to conform to specific gender norms, such as being seen as solely vocalists or performers, while men dominated positions of power and influence. Celia Cruz challenged these expectations by becoming not only a renowned singer but also a songwriter, producer, and bandleader. Her multifaceted talent and refusal to be confined to societal norms set a precedent for future generations of female artists.

We will also delve into the unequal treatment and opportunities afforded to women in the music industry. Celia Cruz's experiences shed light on the gender disparities she encountered, including lower pay, limited access to resources, and a lack of recognition for her contributions. Despite these challenges, she persevered, using her voice and platform to advocate for gender equality and inspire other female artists.

Furthermore, we will explore the harmful stereotypes that women in music often face, such as being objectified or reduced to their physical appearance. Celia Cruz's refusal to conform to these stereotypes, instead focusing on her talent and passion, challenged societal expectations and paved the way for a more inclusive and diverse music industry.

By examining gender inequality and stereotypes in the music industry through the lens of Celia Cruz's career, we hope to shed light on the systemic challenges faced by women in music and inspire a conversation about the importance of equal opportunities and representation for all artists. Celia Cruz's defiance against gender norms and her unwavering commitment to her craft serve as a testament to the power of resilience and determination in the face of adversity.

Join us as we delve into the fascinating world of Celia Cruz and explore the impact of gender inequality and stereotypes in the music industry. Together, let us challenge the status quo and strive for a more inclusive and equitable future for all musicians.

Celia's Struggles and Triumphs as a Female Artist

In a male-dominated industry, Celia Cruz defied all odds and emerged as one of the most influential and revered female artists in history. Her journey was not without its challenges, but Celia's resilience and talent ultimately led to triumphs that would shape the course of Afro-Cuban music and inspire generations to come.

As a female artist in the mid-20th century, Celia faced numerous obstacles. Society had rigid expectations of women, and the music industry was no exception. Yet, she refused to be confined by these limitations. Celia's determination to be heard and to express herself authentically propelled her forward.

One of the defining moments of Celia's career came when she refused to sing for Fidel Castro. This act of defiance showcased her unwavering principles and sparked a political activism that would become a prominent aspect of her legacy. Celia understood the power of her voice and used it to challenge oppressive regimes, becoming a symbol of resistance and freedom.

Celia's influence extended far beyond politics. Her success paved the way for other Latin American divas, empowering them to break barriers and embrace their own unique identities. Celia's Afro-Latina heritage was a crucial element of her music and activism - she celebrated her roots and used her platform to shed light on the Afro-Caribbean experience.

Being a Cuban exile, Celia's artistic expressions were deeply influenced by her experiences. She channeled her pain and longing into her music, creating a fusion of traditional Afro-Cuban rhythms with contemporary sounds. This exploration of her cultural heritage resonated with audiences worldwide and solidified her status as an icon.

As a woman in the music industry, Celia faced gender discrimination, but she refused to be silenced. She defied societal expectations and shattered glass ceilings, proving that women were just as capable of achieving greatness. Her career serves as a testament to the strength and perseverance of women in music.

Celia's refusal to perform for Fidel Castro was not just an act of political resistance, but also a form of cultural resistance. Through her music, she preserved and celebrated the rich traditions of Afro-Cuban culture, even in the face of adversity. Her refusal became a rallying cry for others who sought to preserve their cultural heritage in the midst of oppression.

Celia's migration from Cuba to the United States also played a significant role in shaping her music. The influence of different cultures and musical styles can be heard in her eclectic sound, which captivated audiences and transcended borders. Her experiences as a migrant artist added a layer of complexity and depth to her work, making her a true global icon.

Celia's music was deeply rooted in Afro-Caribbean influences. She drew inspiration from the rhythms and melodies of her homeland, infusing them with her own unique style and energy. This fusion of Afro-Cuban and contemporary sounds revolutionized the genre and solidified her place as the "Queen of Salsa."

The legacy of Celia Cruz is one that continues to resonate today. Her impact on the Afro-Cuban music scene and beyond is immeasurable. Her voice and spirit live on, inspiring future generations of artists to break boundaries, celebrate their heritage, and use their platforms to create positive change.

Celia's struggles and triumphs as a female artist serve as a powerful reminder of the strength and resilience of women in the face of adversity. Her refusal to be silenced, her unwavering commitment to her principles, and her immense talent have left an indelible mark on the world of music and beyond.

Breaking Glass Ceilings and Empowering Future Female Musicians

Celia Cruz: The Defiant Voice of Afro-Cuban Music

In the male-dominated world of music, Celia Cruz emerged as a trailblazer, breaking glass ceilings and empowering future female musicians. Throughout her career, she shattered stereotypes, defied societal expectations, and left an indelible mark on the music industry. Her resilience, passion, and unwavering commitment to her craft make her a true icon, not just in Afro-Cuban music but also as a symbol of female empowerment.

Celia Cruz's refusal to sing for Fidel Castro showcased her unwavering commitment to her principles and her role as a political activist. She understood the power of her voice and used it to stand up against a dictator, sending a powerful message to others in the industry. This act of defiance not only solidified her status as a symbol of resistance but also paved the way for future artists to use their platform for political activism.

Her influence on the rise of Latin American female singers cannot be understated. Celia Cruz broke barriers and opened doors for women in the music industry, inspiring a new generation of divas. Her impact on the diva culture is undeniable, as she showed the world that women could be powerful, confident, and unapologetically themselves.

As a Cuban exile, Celia Cruz's experiences shaped her artistic expressions. Her music became a reflection of the struggles and triumphs of the Cuban exile community, resonating with audiences worldwide. Through her songs, she connected with the diaspora, providing a voice for those who had been silenced.

Celia Cruz's Afro-Latina identity played a significant role in her music and activism. She embraced her heritage and used her platform to celebrate Afro-Caribbean culture, challenging societal norms and promoting inclusivity. Her Afro-Caribbean musical influences were evident in her unique style, blending traditional Cuban rhythms with modern sounds.

Throughout her career, Celia Cruz faced numerous challenges that women in the music industry continue to confront. From gender bias to unequal opportunities, she fought against the odds and proved that talent knows no gender. Her perseverance and success serve as an inspiration to aspiring female musicians, encouraging them to pursue their dreams fearlessly.

Celia Cruz's refusal to perform for Fidel Castro was not only an act of defiance but also a form of cultural resistance against the oppressive Cuban regime. She understood the power of her music and used it to preserve her cultural heritage, refusing to be a pawn in the dictator's game. Her bold stance inspired others to use their art as a means of resistance and cultural preservation.

The influence of migration on Celia Cruz's music cannot be overlooked. As a migrant artist, she used her experiences to infuse her music with a sense of longing, nostalgia, and hope. Her songs became anthems for those who had left their homeland, providing solace and a connection to their roots.

Celia Cruz's legacy and impact on the Afro-Cuban music scene and beyond are profound. Her music continues to resonate with audiences of all backgrounds, transcending borders and language barriers. She will forever be remembered as a pioneer, a symbol of female empowerment, and a defiant voice that shattered glass ceilings for future generations of female musicians.

Celia's Advocacy for Women's Rights in the Music Industry

Celia Cruz's impact on the music industry extends far beyond her powerful voice and vibrant stage presence. Throughout her career, she was a fierce advocate for women's rights, using her platform to challenge gender inequalities in the music industry. From fighting for equal opportunities to highlighting the struggles faced by female artists, Celia paved the way for future generations of women in music.

In a male-dominated industry, Celia Cruz defied expectations and shattered glass ceilings. She faced numerous challenges and obstacles along her journey, but she never allowed these to hinder her passion and determination. Celia's refusal to conform to societal norms and expectations made her a force to be reckoned with.

One of the ways Celia advocated for women's rights in the music industry was by demanding equal opportunities and recognition. She firmly believed that talent should be the sole determinant of success, regardless of gender. Celia fought tirelessly to ensure that female artists received the same opportunities, pay, and respect as their male counterparts.

Moreover, Celia used her music and performances as a platform to address gender inequalities. Through her lyrics and stage presence, she challenged traditional gender roles and stereotypes, encouraging women to embrace their power and celebrate their individuality. Celia became a symbol of strength and empowerment for women across the globe.

Additionally, Celia Cruz's advocacy for women's rights extended beyond the music industry. She used her fame and influence to support various women's organizations and initiatives, championing causes such as reproductive rights, domestic violence prevention, and equal access to education. Celia understood the importance of using her platform for social change and was dedicated to uplifting women from all walks of life.

Celia Cruz's advocacy for women's rights in the music industry continues to inspire and empower. Her fearless pursuit of gender equality set a precedent for future generations of female artists, encouraging them to challenge the status quo and demand the respect they deserve. Celia's legacy serves as a reminder that music has the power to effect change, and that women have an integral role to play in shaping the industry.

As we reflect on Celia's remarkable career and her unwavering dedication to women's rights, it is clear that her impact extends far beyond the Afro-Cuban music scene. She was a trailblazer, a pioneer, and a true icon in her advocacy for gender equality. Celia Cruz's legacy serves as a testament to the power of music and the strength of women in their fight for equality.

Chapter 8: Cultural Resistance: Analyzing how Celia Cruz's Refusal to Perform for Fidel Castro was an Act of Cultural Resistance against the Cuban Regime

Role of Artists in Cultural Resistance Movements

Artists have always played a vital role in cultural resistance movements, using their creative expressions to challenge oppressive systems and advocate for change. In the case of the legendary Afro-Cuban singer, Celia Cruz, her refusal to sing for dictator Fidel Castro stands as a powerful example of the artist's role in political activism and cultural resistance.

Cruz's defiance against Castro was not merely a personal decision; it was a statement of solidarity with the Cuban people who were suffering under an authoritarian regime. By refusing to perform for Castro, Cruz used her voice and platform to amplify the voices of those who were silenced and oppressed.

Cruz's act of resistance was not without consequences. She faced backlash and threats from the Cuban government, which eventually led to her leaving her homeland behind and seeking exile in the United States. However, her decision to prioritize her principles over personal safety showcases the unwavering commitment of artists to challenge unjust systems.

Beyond her refusal to sing for Castro, Cruz's entire career can be seen as a form of cultural resistance. Born and raised in a society that often marginalized Afro-Cuban voices, Cruz used her music to celebrate her African heritage and challenge the prevailing societal norms. Through her vibrant performances and powerful lyrics, she defied stereotypes, broke down barriers, and paved the way for future generations of Afro-Latinx artists.

Cruz's influence extended far beyond the realm of music. She became an iconic figure, not only for her contributions to Afro-Cuban music but also for her activism and advocacy. She used her platform to raise awareness about the struggles faced by marginalized communities, particularly women and Afro-Latinas. Through her music and activism, she inspired countless individuals to embrace their identities and fight for social justice.

In conclusion, the role of artists in cultural resistance movements cannot be underestimated. Celia Cruz's refusal to sing for Fidel Castro and her broader career serve as a testament to the power of artistic expression in challenging oppressive systems and advocating for change. Her legacy continues to inspire artists and activists around the world, reminding us of the transformative potential of art in the face of adversity.

Celia's Decision as a Symbolic Act of Defiance

In the annals of music history, there are few figures as defiant and influential as Celia Cruz. Her refusal to sing for dictator Fidel Castro stands as a symbolic act of defiance that resonates far beyond the realms of music and politics. It represents a bold statement of personal integrity and a refusal to compromise one's principles.

Celia's decision to turn her back on Castro was not made lightly. As a native of Cuba, she understood the power and reach of the regime. However, she also recognized the importance of standing up for what she believed in, even at great personal cost. By refusing to perform for Castro, Celia asserted her independence and unwillingness to be a pawn in a political game.

This act of defiance had far-reaching implications, not just for Celia but for the Afro-Cuban music scene as a whole. It signaled a break from the traditional ties between musicians and the Cuban government, and opened the door for other artists to follow suit. Celia's refusal to sing for Castro became a rallying cry for those who sought to challenge the regime and fight for freedom of expression.

Beyond its political significance, Celia's decision also had a profound impact on the music industry. By taking a stand, she demonstrated the power of art as a tool for social change. Her refusal to compromise her beliefs inspired a generation of musicians to use their platform to speak out against injustice. Celia became a beacon of hope for those who felt marginalized and silenced, showing them that their voices mattered and could make a difference.

Celia's act of defiance also paved the way for other Latin American female singers to rise to prominence. She shattered the glass ceiling and challenged the male-dominated music industry, proving that women could be both talented and powerful. Her influence on the diva culture cannot be overstated, as she set a new standard for female artists and inspired countless others to follow in her footsteps.

In conclusion, Celia's decision to refuse to sing for Fidel Castro was not just a personal choice, but a symbolic act of defiance with far-reaching implications. It represented a break from the traditional ties between musicians and the Cuban government, and inspired a generation of artists to use their platform for social change. Celia's legacy as a defiant voice of Afro-Cuban music will forever be remembered and celebrated.

The Impact of Celia's Decision on the Cuban Regime

In the subchapter titled "The Impact of Celia's Decision on the Cuban Regime," we delve into the profound effects of Celia Cruz's decision to refuse to sing for dictator Fidel Castro. This decision not only showcased her defiance and unwavering principles, but it also had far-reaching consequences that reverberated throughout the Cuban regime.

Celia Cruz's refusal to perform for Fidel Castro was a powerful act of political activism. By taking a stand against the dictator, she became a symbol of resistance and a voice for the oppressed. Her decision sent shockwaves through the Cuban music industry and challenged the status quo. It highlighted the power of artists to use their platform to speak out against injustice and oppression.

Furthermore, Celia's bold stance had a significant impact on the Afro-Cuban music scene and the genre as a whole. Her refusal to sing for Castro was a catalyst for change, leading to a reevaluation of the relationship between musicians and the Cuban regime. It inspired other artists to question and challenge the government's control over their artistic expression.

Celia Cruz's decision also had implications for the broader Latin American diva culture. Her refusal to align herself with the Cuban regime paved the way for other female singers to assert their autonomy and resist political pressure. Her actions empowered a new generation of Latin American women to use their voices to advocate for change and stand up against oppression.

In addition to her political impact, Celia Cruz's decision also shed light on the experiences of Cuban exiles. As a prominent figure in the exile community, her refusal to perform for Castro represented the struggles and sacrifices of those who had fled the regime. It became a symbol of the Cuban exile experience and the resilience of those who had been forced to leave their homeland.

Ultimately, Celia Cruz's decision to refuse to sing for Fidel Castro was not just a personal choice but a powerful act of cultural resistance. It embodied the spirit of defiance and the refusal to be silenced. Her legacy as a political activist and her impact on the Afro-Cuban music scene and beyond continue to resonate to this day. Celia Cruz's unwavering determination and courage serve as an inspiration for artists and activists alike, reminding us of the transformative power of music and the importance of standing up for what we believe in.

Legacy of Celia's Cultural Resistance

Celia Cruz, the iconic Afro-Cuban singer, left behind an unparalleled legacy of cultural resistance that continues to inspire and empower people around the world. Her refusal to sing for Fidel Castro, the dictator of Cuba, was a bold act that showcased her unwavering commitment to her principles and her dedication to fighting for freedom and justice. This subchapter delves into the profound impact of Celia's cultural resistance and its lasting effects on various aspects of society.

Celia Cruz's defiance of Fidel Castro's regime was not just an act of political activism, but also a testament to her unwavering dedication to her art. By refusing to perform for Castro, she demonstrated the power of music as a tool for political expression and resistance. Her actions paved the way for other artists to use their platform to challenge oppressive regimes and advocate for change.

Moreover, Celia's refusal to sing for Castro had a significant impact on the rise of Latin American female singers and the diva culture. She shattered gender stereotypes and became a symbol of empowerment for women in the music industry. Her boldness and charisma inspired countless female artists to strive for greatness and demand equal recognition and opportunities.

Celia Cruz's experiences as a Cuban exile greatly influenced her artistic expressions. Through her music, she expressed the pain, longing, and resilience of her people who were forced to leave their homeland. She became the voice of the Cuban diaspora, channeling their collective experiences into powerful melodies that resonated with audiences worldwide.

Her Afro-Latina identity played a crucial role in shaping her music and activism. Celia celebrated her African roots and embraced her heritage, becoming a symbol of Afro-Caribbean pride. She challenged societal norms and fought against racial discrimination, using her music as a vehicle for promoting inclusivity and unity.

Celia Cruz's refusal to perform for Fidel Castro was an act of cultural resistance that transcended borders and inspired others to stand up against oppressive regimes. Her legacy serves as a reminder that art can be a powerful tool for social change and that artists have a responsibility to use their platform to fight for justice and equality.

In conclusion, Celia Cruz's cultural resistance left an indelible mark on the Afro-Cuban music scene and beyond. Her refusal to sing for Fidel Castro showcased her unwavering commitment to her principles and her dedication to fighting for freedom and justice. Through her music and activism, she became a symbol of empowerment for women, a voice for the Cuban exile community, and a champion of Afro-Latina identity. Celia's legacy continues to inspire artists and activists to use their platform to challenge oppressive systems and advocate for positive change in the world.

Chapter 9: Music and Migration: Examining the Influence of Migration on Celia Cruz's Music and her Experiences as a Migrant Artist

The Impact of Migration on Celia's Life and Career

Migration played a significant role in shaping the life and career of Celia Cruz, the defiant voice of Afro-Cuban music. Born and raised in Havana, Cuba, Celia's journey as an artist and activist was deeply intertwined with her experiences as a migrant. Her migration from Cuba to the United States not only transformed her life but also had a profound impact on her music, activism, and identity.

When Celia and her husband, Pedro Knight, left Cuba in 1960, they were forced to leave behind their families, friends, and the familiar rhythms of their homeland. This forced departure marked the beginning of a new chapter in Celia's life, one filled with both challenges and opportunities. In her new home of the United States, Celia had to navigate a different culture and language, but she was determined to use her voice to make a difference.

As a migrant artist, Celia faced numerous hurdles in her career. She had to prove herself in a new music scene that was unfamiliar with Afro-Cuban rhythms. However, her unique style and powerful voice quickly captivated audiences, and she soon became a trailblazer for Afro-Cuban music in the United States and beyond. Her music became a bridge between her Cuban roots and her new American identity, and she used it to celebrate her heritage and bring people together.

Migration also influenced Celia's activism. Her refusal to sing for Fidel Castro was a powerful act of political resistance, rooted in her experiences as a migrant. Celia understood the importance of using her platform to speak out against injustice, and she became a symbol of hope for those who sought freedom from oppressive regimes. Through her music and activism, she became a voice for the voiceless, empowering others to stand up for their rights.

Celia's migration experience also shaped her Afro-Latina identity. As a black woman in a predominantly white industry, she faced discrimination and prejudice. However, she embraced her Afro-Cuban heritage and used it as a source of strength and empowerment. Celia's music and performances were a celebration of her African roots, challenging societal norms and inspiring others to embrace their own identities.

The impact of migration on Celia's life and career cannot be overstated. It fueled her determination, creativity, and resilience. Her experiences as a migrant artist shaped her music, activism, and identity, leaving a lasting legacy on the Afro-Cuban music scene and beyond. Celia Cruz will forever be remembered as a trailblazer, a cultural icon, and a defiant voice that refused to be silenced. Her story serves as a reminder of the power of migration and the indomitable spirit of those who dare to defy the odds.

Adaptation and Integration in a New Cultural Setting

In the subchapter "Adaptation and Integration in a New Cultural Setting" of the book "Celia Cruz: The Defiant Voice of Afro-Cuban Music," we delve into the remarkable journey of Celia Cruz as she navigated the challenges of adapting and integrating into a new cultural setting. This chapter explores how Cruz's Afro-Cuban roots and her experiences as a migrant artist influenced her music, activism, and ultimately, her legacy.

As an Afro-Cuban singer who refused to sing for dictator Fidel Castro, Cruz's decision to defy the regime placed her at the forefront of political activism. We examine the significance of her refusal and delve into her role as a political activist, shedding light on the courage and determination she displayed. Cruz's refusal to perform for Castro was not only an act of cultural resistance against the Cuban regime, but it also highlighted the power of music as a tool for social change.

Furthermore, we explore Cruz's Afro-Latina identity and the profound impact it had on her music and activism. Her Afro-Caribbean influences are examined in detail, showcasing how her unique style and distinct voice contributed to the rise of Latin American female singers and the diva culture. Moreover, we investigate the experiences of Cuban exiles, including Cruz, and how their forced migration influenced their artistic expressions.

The challenges faced by women in the music industry are also explored through the lens of Cruz's career. We analyze the barriers she encountered and the ways in which she shattered stereotypes, empowering future generations of female artists. Cruz's resilience and determination serve as an inspiration to women in music, highlighting the importance of breaking societal norms and striving for gender equality.

Finally, we discuss Cruz's lasting legacy and impact on the Afro-Cuban music scene and beyond. Her contributions to the genre and her defiant voice continue to resonate with audiences worldwide, cementing her as a legendary figure in music history. We delve into how migration influenced her music and her experiences as a migrant artist, showcasing the powerful connection between music and the migrant experience.

In the subchapter "Adaptation and Integration in a New Cultural Setting," readers will gain a comprehensive understanding of how Celia Cruz's journey as an Afro-Cuban singer shaped her music, activism, and legacy. Her refusal to sing for Fidel Castro, her Afro-Latina identity, and her role as a trailblazer for women in music are all explored in detail, shedding light on the indelible mark she left on the Afro-Cuban music scene and beyond.

Influence of Celia's Migration Experience on her Music

One of the most profound aspects of Celia Cruz's life was her experience as a migrant artist. Born and raised in Cuba, Celia made the difficult decision to leave her homeland in the midst of political turmoil and seek a new life in the United States. This migration had a significant impact on her music and shaped her career in ways that would forever change the Afro-Cuban music scene.

Celia's migration experience brought with it a sense of longing and nostalgia for her homeland. This longing is evident in many of her songs, where she sings of love for Cuba and a yearning to return. Through her music, Celia was able to connect with other Cuban exiles who shared similar experiences and emotions. Her songs became anthems of hope and resilience for a community longing for their homeland, and her powerful voice became a symbol of strength and unity.

Furthermore, Celia's migration experience allowed her to blend her Afro-Cuban roots with the vibrant music scene in the United States. In New York City, Celia was exposed to a myriad of musical genres, including jazz, soul, and salsa. She embraced these influences and incorporated them into her own unique style, creating a fusion that would revolutionize Afro-Cuban music. Celia's music became a bridge between cultures, attracting audiences from different backgrounds and bringing Afro-Cuban rhythms to the forefront of the global music scene.

Additionally, Celia's migration experience fueled her passion for political activism. As a staunch opponent of Fidel Castro's regime, she refused to sing for the dictator, a decision that would have lasting implications for her career. Celia's defiance against the Cuban regime was a powerful act of resistance, and her refusal to compromise her principles only further solidified her status as a cultural icon.

In conclusion, Celia Cruz's migration experience played a pivotal role in shaping her music and career. It allowed her to channel her longing for Cuba into powerful songs of hope and resilience, while also exposing her to new musical influences that would redefine the Afro-Cuban music scene. Moreover, her migration experience fueled her political activism and solidified her status as a cultural icon. Celia's legacy continues to inspire generations of artists and her impact on the Afro-Cuban music scene and beyond is immeasurable.

Celia's Representation of the Migrant Experience

In the subchapter titled "Celia's Representation of the Migrant Experience," we delve into the captivating journey of Celia Cruz, the iconic Afro-Cuban singer, and her profound connection to the migrant experience. Celia's story resonates not only with those interested in her remarkable career but also with individuals exploring the broader themes of migration, identity, and resilience.

Born in Havana, Cuba, Celia Cruz became a symbol of the Afro-Cuban diaspora, a testament to the strength and determination of those who leave their homeland in search of a better life. As she embarked on her musical journey, Celia's experiences as a migrant artist shaped her artistic expression and contributed to her unique voice within the Afro-Cuban music genre.

Celia's migration to the United States in 1960, following the Cuban Revolution, marked a turning point in her career and life. Her decision to leave behind her beloved Cuba and refuse to sing for Fidel Castro demonstrated her unwavering commitment to her principles and her refusal to compromise her artistic integrity. This act of defiance against a dictator not only solidified her position as a political activist but also exemplified her role as a vocal advocate for freedom and human rights.

Throughout her career, Celia's music served as a powerful medium to explore the complexities of her Afro-Latina identity. Her songs celebrated her African heritage and embraced her cultural roots, challenging societal norms and paving the way for future generations of Afro-Latina artists. Celia's music became a platform for cultural resistance, an affirmation of her identity, and a source of empowerment for marginalized communities.

Furthermore, Celia's experiences as a migrant artist brought to light the challenges faced by women in the music industry. Her relentless pursuit of success and refusal to be silenced served as an inspiration for aspiring female musicians, breaking barriers and shattering stereotypes.

Celia's legacy extends far beyond the Afro-Cuban music scene. Her influence played a pivotal role in the rise of Latin American female singers and the development of the diva culture. Her impact continues to resonate today, as her music and activism serve as a source of inspiration for artists worldwide.

In this subchapter, we explore the profound connection between Celia Cruz and the migrant experience. We delve into her music, her activism, and her unwavering determination, shedding light on the challenges faced by migrants and the transformative power of art and music in navigating the complexities of identity and belonging. Celia Cruz's story serves as a testament to the resilience and strength of those who dare to pursue their dreams, regardless of the obstacles they encounter along the way.

Chapter 10: Afro-Caribbean Influences: Investigating the Afro-Caribbean Musical Influences in Celia Cruz's Work and their Impact on her Style

Afro-Caribbean Music and its Variations

In the vibrant realm of Afro-Caribbean music, a rich tapestry of rhythmic beats, soulful melodies, and infectious dance moves intertwine to create a sound that resonates with the hearts of millions. This subchapter delves into the captivating world of Afro-Caribbean music and explores its variations, with a particular focus on the legendary Celia Cruz and her significant contributions to the genre.

From the lively streets of Cuba to the sun-soaked shores of the Caribbean, Afro-Caribbean music encompasses a vast array of styles and influences. Rooted in the African diaspora, this genre blends indigenous rhythms with elements of jazz, salsa, reggae, and more, forging a unique sonic landscape that captivates listeners worldwide.

Celia Cruz, often referred to as the Queen of Salsa, played a pivotal role in popularizing Afro-Caribbean music and introducing it to global audiences. Her powerful voice, commanding stage presence, and infectious energy breathed new life into the genre, revolutionizing the way people perceived and appreciated Afro-Caribbean music.

This subchapter explores the impact of Afro-Cuban music on Celia Cruz's career and delves into her contributions to the genre. It sheds light on her unparalleled ability to infuse traditional Afro-Caribbean rhythms with contemporary elements, thus creating a sound that transcended cultural boundaries and spoke to the hearts of people from all walks of life.

Additionally, this subchapter examines Celia Cruz's refusal to sing for Fidel Castro and her role as a political activist. It explores how her decision to use her voice as a means of resistance against the Cuban regime made her a symbol of defiance and a beacon of hope for those who longed for freedom and justice.

Furthermore, this subchapter delves into Celia Cruz's influence on the rise of Latin American female singers and her impact on the diva culture. It highlights how her unwavering determination, unapologetic authenticity, and trailblazing spirit shattered glass ceilings and paved the way for future generations of Latin American divas.

Moreover, this subchapter investigates the experiences of Cuban exiles, including Celia Cruz, and their impact on their artistic expressions. It explores how the pain of displacement, longing for home, and the quest for identity shaped their music, creating a powerful mirror that reflected the resilience and strength of the Afro-Cuban community.

In conclusion, Afro-Caribbean music, with its myriad variations and influences, is a testament to the rich cultural heritage of the African diaspora. Celia Cruz, with her defiant voice and unwavering spirit, not only left an indelible mark on the Afro-Cuban music scene but also inspired countless artists and activists worldwide. Her legacy continues to resonate, reminding us of the transformative power of music and its ability to bring people together, drive social change, and celebrate the beauty of diversity.

Celia's Exploration and Incorporation of Afro-Caribbean Rhythms

In the realm of Afro-Cuban music, Celia Cruz stands out as a trailblazer who fearlessly explored and incorporated Afro-Caribbean rhythms into her music. Her journey as an artist was marked by a deep appreciation for her African roots and a commitment to celebrating and preserving the rich musical traditions of the Afro-Caribbean diaspora.

Celia's exploration of Afro-Caribbean rhythms began at a young age in her native Cuba. Growing up in a vibrant musical environment, she was exposed to a variety of musical genres, including son, rumba, and mambo. These genres, with their African origins and rhythmic complexities, captivated her and became the foundation of her artistic expression.

As her career progressed, Celia's passion for Afro-Caribbean rhythms only grew stronger. She fearlessly experimented with blending different musical styles, infusing her music with elements of Afro-Cuban, Afro-Puerto Rican, and Afro-Dominican rhythms. This fusion created a unique sound that transcended borders and resonated with audiences worldwide.

Celia's incorporation of Afro-Caribbean rhythms was not just a musical choice; it was also a political statement. By embracing and promoting the music of her African ancestors, she challenged the Eurocentric norms that dominated the music industry. In doing so, she became a symbol of cultural resistance, using her music as a powerful tool to assert her identity and promote the Afro-Latina experience.

Her exploration and incorporation of Afro-Caribbean rhythms also had a profound impact on the genre itself. Celia's boldness and innovation inspired a new generation of Afro-Cuban musicians and paved the way for the Afro-Cuban music renaissance that followed. Her influence can be heard in the works of artists such as Issac Delgado, Albita Rodriguez, and many others who continue to carry the torch of Afro-Caribbean music.

Today, Celia Cruz's legacy as the defiant voice of Afro-Cuban music lives on. Her music continues to captivate audiences, and her contributions to the genre are celebrated worldwide. Through her exploration and incorporation of Afro-Caribbean rhythms, Celia Cruz not only left an indelible mark on the music industry but also became a symbol of resilience, cultural pride, and the power of music to transcend boundaries.

Collaboration with Afro-Caribbean Artists

One of the defining aspects of Celia Cruz's career was her collaboration with Afro-Caribbean artists, which played a significant role in shaping her unique style and sound. Throughout her illustrious career, Cruz worked with numerous musicians from the Afro-Caribbean community, blending different musical traditions and genres to create a truly groundbreaking fusion.

Cruz's collaborations with Afro-Caribbean artists allowed her to explore and incorporate various elements of Afro-Cuban, Afro-Latin, and Afro-Caribbean music into her repertoire. These collaborations not only enriched her music but also served as a platform for cultural exchange and celebration of African heritage in the Caribbean.

One notable collaboration was with the legendary Puerto Rican musician Tito Puente, often referred to as the "King of Latin Music." Their partnership resulted in a series of hit records and performances that showcased the vibrant rhythms of Afro-Caribbean music, such as mambo, salsa, and cha-cha-cha. Cruz's powerful voice combined with Puente's innovative arrangements created an irresistible and infectious sound that captivated audiences worldwide.

Another significant collaboration in Cruz's career was with the Jamaican reggae artist Bob Marley. This unexpected pairing brought together two musical giants from different genres and cultural backgrounds. The result was a remarkable fusion of reggae and Afro-Cuban rhythms, as showcased in their iconic duet "Bemba Colora."

Cruz's collaborations with Afro-Caribbean artists not only pushed the boundaries of music but also challenged societal norms. By working closely with artists from different backgrounds, she broke down cultural barriers and fostered a spirit of unity and inclusiveness. This collaboration was a testament to her belief in the power of music to transcend borders and bring people together.

Furthermore, Cruz's collaborations with Afro-Caribbean artists highlighted the rich and diverse musical heritage of the African diaspora in the Caribbean. Through her music, she celebrated the contributions of Afro-Caribbean artists to the global music scene, helping to elevate their voices and showcase their talent to a wider audience.

In conclusion, Celia Cruz's collaborations with Afro-Caribbean artists were instrumental in shaping her unique sound and style. These partnerships not only resulted in groundbreaking music but also fostered cultural exchange and celebration of African heritage in the Caribbean. By collaborating with artists from different backgrounds, Cruz challenged societal norms and united people through the power of music. Her legacy as a collaborator with Afro-Caribbean artists continues to inspire and influence musicians today, ensuring that her contributions to the Afro-Cuban and Afro-Caribbean music scenes will never be forgotten.

Influence of Afro-Caribbean Music on Celia's Vocal Techniques and Performance Style

Celia Cruz, often hailed as the Queen of Salsa, was not only a powerful vocalist and performer but also an influential figure in the Afro-Cuban music scene. One of the key factors that shaped her unique vocal techniques and performance style was the profound influence of Afro-Caribbean music.

Afro-Caribbean music, with its rich blend of African and Caribbean rhythms, played a significant role in shaping the sound and style of Celia Cruz. Growing up in Havana, Cuba, Celia was exposed to a variety of musical genres, including rumba, son, and Afro-Cuban jazz. These genres were deeply rooted in African traditions and carried the vibrant energy and rhythms of the Afro-Caribbean culture.

Celia's exposure to Afro-Caribbean music from an early age had a transformative effect on her vocal techniques. She adopted the rhythmic patterns and melodic structures commonly found in Afro-Caribbean genres, infusing them into her own songs. Her voice, characterized by its powerful and passionate delivery, was influenced by the soulful melodies and vocal improvisation techniques commonly used in Afro-Caribbean music.

Furthermore, Afro-Caribbean music also shaped Celia's performance style. The energetic and syncopated beats inherent in this genre inspired her dynamic stage presence and infectious dance moves. Celia's performances were not just about singing; they were a complete sensory experience, with her vibrant costumes, expressive gestures, and charismatic personality captivating audiences worldwide.

Celia's incorporation of Afro-Caribbean musical elements into her work not only made her an icon in the Afro-Cuban music scene but also helped popularize the genre on a global scale. Her fusion of Afro-Cuban rhythms with modern salsa and Latin jazz created a unique sound that appealed to a wide audience, transcending cultural boundaries.

Celia Cruz's influence on the Afro-Cuban music scene and beyond cannot be overstated. Her mastery of Afro-Caribbean vocal techniques and performance style set her apart as a trailblazer in the industry. Her ability to infuse her music with the soul and spirit of Afro-Caribbean rhythms continues to inspire and influence generations of musicians to this day.

In conclusion, the influence of Afro-Caribbean music on Celia Cruz's vocal techniques and performance style cannot be underestimated. Her exposure to the vibrant rhythms and melodies of this genre shaped her unique sound and stage presence, making her a legendary figure in the Afro-Cuban music scene. Celia's fusion of Afro-Caribbean elements with modern genres helped popularize the genre on a global scale and cemented her status as a true icon in the world of music.

Chapter 11: Legacy and Impact: Discussing the Lasting Legacy of Celia Cruz and her Impact on the Afro-Cuban Music Scene and Beyond

Celia's Influence on Future Generations of

Celia's Influence on Future Generations of Afro-Cuban Music

Celia Cruz, the defiant voice of Afro-Cuban music, left an indelible mark on future generations of musicians, not only in her native Cuba but also across the globe. Her fearless approach to music and her refusal to conform to the constraints of political regimes set her apart as a trailblazer and an inspiration.

Celia's influence on Afro-Cuban music can be seen through her unwavering dedication to preserving the roots of the genre. She incorporated traditional Afro-Cuban rhythms and melodies into her music, infusing it with a unique blend of African and Latin influences. This fusion not only added depth and richness to her songs but also served as a catalyst for the evolution of Afro-Cuban music.

Her contributions to the genre extended beyond her own music. Celia mentored and collaborated with emerging artists, nurturing their talent and guiding them to success. She believed in the power of supporting and uplifting others, and this legacy of mentorship has continued to shape the Afro-Cuban music scene.

Furthermore, Celia's refusal to sing for Fidel Castro showcased her unwavering commitment to her principles and her role as a political activist. Her act of defiance resonated deeply with others who were also oppressed by oppressive regimes, inspiring them to use their art as a form of resistance. Celia's refusal to compromise her beliefs set a powerful example for future generations of musicians, encouraging them to use their platform to effect change.

Celia's influence on the rise of Latin American female singers cannot be overstated. She shattered stereotypes and paved the way for female artists to be seen and heard in a male-dominated industry. Her unapologetic confidence and larger-than-life persona became the blueprint for many Latin American divas who followed in her footsteps.

Beyond her musical contributions, Celia's Afro-Latina identity played a significant role in her activism and her music. She proudly embraced her African heritage, using her voice as a platform to celebrate and uplift Afro-Cuban culture. Her Afro-Latina identity was not just a personal expression; it was a statement of empowerment for marginalized communities.

In conclusion, Celia Cruz's influence on future generations of Afro-Cuban music cannot be overstated. Her unwavering dedication to preserving the roots of the genre, her fearless activism, and her role as a mentor and inspiration continue to shape the music industry today. Celia's legacy as the defiant voice of Afro-Cuban music lives on, impacting the cultural landscape and inspiring musicians for years to come.

www.ingramcontent.com/pod-product-compliance
Lightning Source LLC
Chambersburg PA
CBHW022051150726
47990CB00003B/1048